To- Will, Tiffrall & re.
Thank Yu
Fork Chape
Appreciated.
Merry Christmas!

Everything Gonna
Be Alright!

Bob Willis

Bob Willis

VANTAGE PRESS
New York

The recipe contained in this book has been selected and written down by the author. The recipe herein has not been tested by the publisher.

Scripture quotations are from the New Revised Standard Version of the Bible, copyright © 1989 by the Division of Christian Education of the National Council of Churches of Christ in the USA. Used by permission. All rights reserved.

The author's essay "Can Anyone Out There Fix This Phone?" was previously published in *U.S. News and World Report* and *North Area News,* his essay "The Whittemore Spring" was published in *The Upper Room;* and his poem "The Mourning Trees" was published in *Diamonds and Pearls.*

FIRST EDITION

Copyright © 2006 by Bob Willis

Published by Vantage Press, Inc.
419 Park Ave. South, New York, NY 10016

Manufactured in the United States of America
ISBN: 0-533-15235-6

Library of Congress Catalog Card No.: 2005903730

0 9 8 7 6 5 4 3 2

To Phoebe;
My Wife,
My Friend,
My Confidante
and
My Love

And

In Memory of
"Papa Joe"
My Trusted Barnabas

Contents

From the Author to the Reader

As early as I can recall, I remember the "fire and brimstone" preachers who preached until they almost lost their voices. They were "Fundamentalist" although at the time they did not call themselves "Fundamentalist." They were good people, but the theology was designed to scare the hell out of you so you would repent and go to heaven. Guilt, fear, and the wrath of God were served up each Sunday. The preachers were never seminary-trained. I guess the thought was "you either are or you ain't! You can't be trained to be a preacher!"

That was another life, another era. For many years I stayed away from the church. It just didn't work for me. But, with the passage of time, things changed, and I eventually grew into new understandings of faith matters. I would never claim that all my views are correct, but they are what I believe.

I retired as a United Methodist Minister of the North Georgia Conference in 2003, before which I had the privilege of serving churches for thirty years. Now, sitting in my office at home in front of the computer, I am surrounded by what my wife refers to as "The Room of Memories." There are notes from people and pictures of family and friends. There are published newspaper articles written long ago. The room is seldom quiet. On the desk are journals that contain sketched notes about people, fishing trips and events along the way. The room is adorned with gifts from friends. Many of the ornaments and trinkets denote trout fishing. On the wall is an aerial photograph of my hometown, Oakman, Georgia. There is a picture of a church I served in my first full-time appointment.

At times the room speaks with a quiet voice of past events, places and people. Well, some of the people would probably not be viewed as righteous souls. A few have been cast as "notorious," but they are all part of my life, and I love them every one. Other times the room speaks with a sad voice because there are memories alive here of people who are no longer in this world. Love is heard and remembered here. There is a picture of a preacher being rescued on the Chattachoochee River by the "River Rescue Team." It seems he was jumping from rock to rock when an ankle was shattered.

As I listen to the memory voices, I realize that memories are a gift. Perhaps they are eternal. They don't age, but I suspect they undergo alterations with the passage of time. They may not always be in the forefront of our mind, but they are there . . . lingering under the surface waiting for the right time to reappear and speak to our consciousness.

This book comes from the room of memories. The people, the places and the observations are interconnected in such a way that they have helped shape my perspective on life. The first essay is the title of the book. A little phrase uttered by a black man long ago has stayed with me over the years. It is a theological statement. I believe you could say it is a statement of hope. It is not a far-flung hope into some magical world where one gets anything and everything they want. But it is that certain hope that regardless of how bad or good, sad or happy, prosperous or poor the circumstances may be, we can get through them. Faith has a way of dealing with life through the tough times as well as the good times. Something about it tells us that we are not alone.

It is my hope that this statement be not taken as an over-simplification, but a statement to be considered in daily life. An important phrase frequently found in the Bible is—"And it came to pass." Nothing stays the same forever. Life and circumstances are continuously changing. Even when the end comes and all the dust of life has settled, we can say with Charlie—"Everything gonna be alright!"

Everything Gonna Be Alright

Years ago in another world and another life, I worked for the Louisville and Nashville R.R. Co. as a freight agent. I worked in most of the depots between Knoxville and Atlanta during this time. Church, religion, and especially theology did not make my favorite top ten list. It now seems so long ago.

While working at Cartersville, Georgia, I met a black man named Charlie who also worked for the railroad. His job was in the freight yard doing maintenance on the train cars and making sure they were in condition to travel. Charlie was a man of few words. People laughed at him, thinking he was a simple man with little education. His favorite phrase in the entire world was, "Everything gonna be alright!" How you doing, Charlie? His response? "Everything gonna be alright!" No matter what the question was, his response was the same. Charlie, is that boxcar ready to go? "Uh huh, everything gonna be alright!"

I remembered thinking, *Charlie, why don't you learn to live in the real world?* I interpreted his response as simple, immature, and foolish. You see, I knew better. I knew that everything was not all right. I knew Charlie's life was tough. He was married and had five children. He had difficulty in making ends meet from one paycheck to another, and discrimination was very much alive in those days. *Everything gonna be alright indeed!* Who was he trying to fool?

One day Charlie and I had a conversation out in the yard while he was on a break. Dressed in his usual greasy overalls and high-top shoes along with the dirty baseball cap that adorned his head, we sat down on the loading platform. I began to question him about his simple, overused phrase. I explained to him that if he would just look around and see the world as it is, he would know that his favorite phrase was trite and meaningless.

Charlie began to speak in a soft voice as though he was afraid someone would overhear our conversation. "Mr. Bob, I trust in my Lord Jesus. I don't look at the world the way it is but how I think Jesus would like for it to be. And you know, no matter how bad things get here, I have a hope that they will be better. And even if they don't get better, I know in my heart that one day when I meet Jesus face to face, they will be better. That's what I believe, Mr. Bob, and I know the day will come when everything gonna be alright!"

Charlie was transformed right before my eyes that day from maintenance man to theologian! I said no more, got up, went back to my office and tried to work. His words would not go away.

The next morning when I got to the office, Charlie was standing outside looking in through the window. I raised the window and he said, "Morning, Mr. Bob. How you doing today?"

I smiled at Charlie. And then I heard myself saying to him, "Hey, Charlie, everything gonna be alright!"

"Amen," he said, and he went about his work.

It's strange how a word or simple phrase uttered by someone you hardly know may stay with you for a lifetime.

Modican-Dean

Like a giant snake moving slowly and gracefully over the landscape, the Coosawattee River meandered through hundreds of acres of rich, fertile land. Corn and cotton were the main crops grown by many black families who lived on this land, which was known as Carter's Quarter. It is now history because Carter's Dam stands towering over this region of used-to-be farmland.

It was in the early 40s. The land was alive with people, mules, and the sound of plows turning the earth, and music—gospel music that lasted most of the day on any given Sunday.

Modican-Dean was a black man who grew up on Carter's Quarter. He seemed too old for the number of years that he had lived. The hard work, sweat, blood and tears had taken their toll. He had a large family. His transportation was a wagon pulled by two mules. Uneducated and very poor in material things, Modican-Dean could be seen sitting proudly aboard his wagon with his family on his way to the store or to church. One thing he knew was hard work because they had met when he was a young boy.

Modican-Dean had worked the land at Carter's Quarter all his life. I guess you could say he had been promoted, as for now, he was in charge of the mules. Rising early in the mornings, he would have the mules out of the barns and hitched up ready for work. After work, he would again take charge of the mules. Daylight was beginning to break. All the men would be gathering, waiting for the time of toil. You could hear early morning small talk and sometimes laughter as they stood around rolling cigarettes, and the aroma of the smoke from Prince Albert, Country Gentleman, or Bull Durham hung heavy in the morning air. With the sun coming up over the river, the time was approaching.

Modican-Dean would walk over to a large, wooden post on which was mounted a bell. A rope hung silently from the bell awaiting the master's hand. In the bib of his overalls was a pocketwatch tethered to him by an old shoestring. Standing by the bell with one hand on the rope and the watch in the other, he surveyed the area in silence as though the world itself depended on his accuracy in timing. At the appointed tick of the watch, Modican-Dean pulled the rope; the bell rang out over the land, setting men and mules in motion. At the dinner hour, he again rang the bell and men and mules ate and rested. Then, he would again set his world in motion, and later call them for an evening's rest. The sound of the bell was clear and distinct and could be heard throughout the river bottoms and adjoining fields.

During the evening meal, Modican-Dean sat at the head of the table, his wife and children gathered with him. The lantern light gave off shadowy, dancing figures around the room. The sound of burning wood in the fireplace and the soft glow of the warm, amber light, made a peaceful setting. At the head of the table sat a proud man, a man who had been blessed with a good wife and many children. The blessing was given by Modican-Dean. He had the respect of his family.

After all, Modican-Dean was the man who pulled the rope . . .

Modican-Dean and Dad

(The rest of the story)

He looked old for his age. The years of hard work had taken a toll on his life. He was still a proud man, a man on whom the badge of honor of hard work was evident. He had been a field worker. "Sharecropper" was a label that had been provided by a culture of the time. He was Modican-Dean, a black man who had worked all his life on Carter's Quarter. He was not a large man, but a muscular man from all the work he had performed over the years. He wore an old floppy hat, overalls, and high top work shoes. Because of his years of faithful dedication to his work, he had been promoted. He was now in charge of all the mules for the field hands. His work also included ringing the large "farm bell" that called people to work and announced the quitting time each day.

My dad was not an educated man by today's standards. But in many ways, he was a man of wisdom and he accepted others regardless of their station in life. Racism was not in his vocabulary. When it came to the question of race, he was ahead of his time. Slowly but surely, my dad evolved into my most beloved hero. It was he who would introduce me to many new and wonderful experiences. One day while we were coon hunting on Slueder Mountain, he pointed out a track on the ground. "You know what that is?" he asked.

"No," I replied.

"That is a deer track. They must be moving back into this part of the country." It was a special moment for me as I knelt down and touched the track with my hand.

My dad was the one who introduced me to the blues music he loved. He would listen to "Randy's Record Shop" on the radio from Gallatin, Tennessee, where blues was played twenty-four hours a day. He also introduced me to Modican-Dean, who became a folk hero to me. Their friendship played an important part in the life of this eight-year-old boy.

Modican-Dean was a proud man. He and his family lived in almost impoverished conditions, but people showed him great respect. Many times I saw him aboard his two-mule wagon, sitting erect as though on a throne. The mules were well kept. Sleek, fat, and strong, they pulled the wagon with matching dignity. This was the only means of transportation for Modican-Dean and his family.

On a workday at Carter's Quarter, he would arise early in the morning and get the mules ready for their job. Harnesses, lines, and plows were made ready before the field hands arrived.

Carter's Quarter was all he knew of the world and his place of work. Hundreds of acres of rich, fertile land had to be tilled, planted, and harvested. The main crops were cotton and corn. When the crops had all been harvested, there was timber to be cut. A sawmill was housed at the base of Carter Mountain. Modican-Dean's duties were year round.

By the time the field hands arrived for work, the mules were harnessed and ready. They would shift their weight from one foot to the other. You could hear the low, guttural sounds they made as they waited for work. Their flanks would quiver in the early morning cold and their breath could be seen shooting from their nostrils. Then, Modican-Dean pulled the rope and rang the bell at the appointed time. After the day's work, he would take care of the mules. He took great pride in his care for the animals.

I recall the Sunday my dad took me to the Carter's Quarter AME Church, a small sanctuary that probably seated no more than seventy-five people. It was my first experience with worship in a Black church. The church had wood-slat pews for seating the congregation. There was no piano or organ. In the chancel area, a lone pulpit occupied center stage. In summer, all the windows would be raised and everyone had a hand-held fan provided by the local funeral home. In the winter, a pot-bellied stove was located at the front center of the church. The sides of the stove and stovepipes burned red hot in an effort to warm the building.

If it was winter, the wood stove was doing its best to keep the congregation warm. The preacher gave a spoken call to worship. Announcements were made. The preacher's Sunday-go-to-meeting clothes consisted of overalls, a white shirt and tie, and work shoes shined with liquid polish. After the announcements, the preacher called on Modican-Dean to lead the congregation in singing hymns. He walked down the center aisle. A chair was placed just outside the chancel area. I watched as my folk-hero carefully seated himself in the cane-bottom chair. *The hymnbooks, where are the hymnbooks?* I thought to myself.

He paused for what seemed like a long time. He was decked out in his usual clothes with the exception of the floppy hat. He had added a white shirt and necktie to his Sunday wardrobe. I noticed that he still had the pocketwatch buried inside the pocket in the bib of his overalls.

He leaned back in the chair with his head tilted upward. Then he began to sing in a soulful tone—"I'm on my way, to Canaan Land, I'm on my way to Canaan Land, I'm on my way to Canaan Land, Praise the Lord, I'm on my way!" And the congregation joined in. It was the most beautiful, harmonic singing that I had ever heard! It lasted for a long time with different words that I didn't know. Something in the way it was sung was so new to me. Even at an early age, I was greatly moved by the sincere, soulful sound.

The morning worship lasted for about two hours. After the preaching service was over, there was time for more singing which filled most of the day. I had never before experienced such a time in church. When the service finally ended, I found myself wishing there was more to come.

As we drove home in dad's old Dodge truck, my mind was racing with excitement. I remembered how difficult it was for me to sit still in our home church. I respected our preacher and our worship services, but now I had discovered something completely different. Sunday after Sunday, I had sat through "hell-fire-and-damnation" services, but this was different. I left the AME Church on top of the world, and everything seemed all right! No guilt, no anxiety, no fear—just a spirit of jubilation filled my young soul . . .

There were many good days of Gospel singing at Carter's Quarter. Each time, my spirit was lifted higher and higher. I asked myself over and over, "What was the difference?" Why did I feel so good after services at the

AME Church? It would take years of life's experiences before I understood some of the answers to those questions.

It was summer. The days were long and hot. Modican-Dean had been to the store at Carter's Quarter to buy supplies for his family. The store was a combination hardware, gas station, post office, and grocery. On his meager income, Modican-Dean did everything in his power to provide for his family. He was a Christian, a hard worker, and above all a family man. His wagon was loaded with food and feed for his animals. Included was a bag of hard rock candy for his children.

I was playing in the backyard when my dad came to me and said, "Get in the truck. We have to go!" I knew something was wrong by the tone of my dad's voice. We got in the truck and headed for Carter's Quarter. No words were spoken on the way. I wondered why my dad was so quiet. As we approached Carter's Quarter, at the place where the road crosses the railroad, he stopped the truck. I will never forget the look on his face.

Then, the words that cut through me like a bitter winter wind—"Modican-Dean is dead."

Dad began to tell me what had happened. Modican-Dean was on his way home with the needed supplies. When he arrived at the railroad crossing, something terrible had happened! As the mules and wagon moved to the crossing, a freight train blew its loud, shrilling whistle. The mules froze in their tracks. Modican-Dean tried desperately to get the animals to move, but they stood their ground. The train was approaching as he shouted, "Get up! Come on, get up!" He never left the mules and wagon.

There was a loud crash! Wagon, mules, supplies, and Modican-Dean went in different directions when the train plowed into them. I looked at the scene and there was a sickening, hard knot in the pit of my stomach. His body had already been removed, food and feed still remained scattered over a wide area. Off to one side, there was a small torn bag with a few remains of hard rock candy.

That was my first taste of real tragedy and loss. Fifty-eight years later, I can still hear the voice of my folk-hero leading the congregation: "I'm on my way, to Canaan Land." And my dad, who accepted all people and had introduced me to Modican-Dean, had grown in stature in my life. And now, as I think about Modican-Dean, my respect for him has grown even more.

After all, he was the man who pulled the rope and sang the songs of hope.

A Man Called John

From my childhood days, I remember an old man by the name of Mr. John Pack, better known as "Brother John." A man short in stature with few visible earthly possessions, "Brother John" lived out his life in Oakman, Georgia. He was a member of a small, rural Holiness Church.

John was a religious man, a holy man who was not ashamed of the Lord. John lived in a small wood-frame house built at the base of a large hill. At the top of the hill, John had an altar made of rocks. There, on his knees, he would pray morning and night. Our home was about six hundred yards from his place of prayer. Despite the distance, you could hear prayers being sent to the throne of God. Even today, I can still recall and hear the prayers of John.

He prayed with great intensity! You could tell by the tone and rhythm of his voice when he was greatly burdened. You could also tell when he had "prayed through" and reached the throne room and claimed the victory.

There were some folks who laughed at Brother John. Of course they thought he was excessive in his praying and worship. John did not mind verbalizing the joy of the Lord.

He was committed to God. He was dedicated and he loved Jesus. He was a mighty man of God!

I remember John and the way he was, and I look at myself and wonder...where are the fiery prophets of old? Where is the voice of the one "crying in the wilderness" today? Where is the enthusiasm? Where is the burden for the souls of other people?

John has been gone a long time now. I miss that gentle and loving soul; I miss seeing the joy he had in his life. I miss Brother John, man of God.

"The wind blows where it chooses, and you hear the sound of it, but you do not know where it comes from or where it goes. So it is with everyone who is born of the Spirit." (John 3:8 NRSV).

Sister Lill

Sister Lilly had always been old. Or, at least she appeared that way to a youngster. She was a woman engaged in serious business. Her appearance denoted that fact: stern, square-faced, heavy eyebrows, hair pulled back tightly into a bun, a dark, long dress, black shoes and never a smile. I do not ever recall hearing Sister Lill laugh. After all, there's no time for trivialities. We must be about the Lord's work.

Sister Lill was known for scaring the hell out of people. She was a staunch Fundamentalist who went about getting souls saved whether a person wanted to be saved or not. One could say that Sister Lill was focused, and nothing would detract her from her mission.

On many occasions I've witnessed her at work during a church service. She would sit in the front of the church so she could view the congregation without much effort. The preachers were all cut from the same cloth. They would preach for an hour or more, and their shirts would be wet with perspiration before the sermon was over. A pitcher of water and a glass, along with a Bible, was always on the pulpit. The only time they were not shouting with a penetrating voices was when they would stop for a moment to swallow a drink of water. (I always thought the water was to wash the fire and brimstone from their parched throats.) Their message although long in duration could be summed up in one short sentence—"turn or burn!"

At the end of the sermon, there would be a long "altar call." This was a time when people were invited to come forward, in public, repent, and be saved. Now this is where Sister Lill ranked supreme, and it was at this point that I always made sure that I sat behind a large person so I could escape the gaze of Sister Lill. As everyone stood to sing the invitational hymn, Sister Lill would survey the congregation. You never wanted to make eye contact with her; anyone who did immediately assumed a "hang-dog" look. That is, head down, hoping that she didn't see you. This posture only added fuel to the fire in Sister Lill. If she saw you in this position, she assumed you were a sinner and needed to be saved.

Sister Lill would leave her pew and make her way to the presumed sinner and begin asking questions like, "Are you lost? Do you want to go to heaven?" Then, grasping an arm, she would gently but forcefully, pull the person away from their seat down to the "mourner's bench" so they could pray through and receive salvation. It mattered not how long you stayed at the mourner's bench; you were required to be there until you could answer Sister Lill in the affirmative. "Yes, I want to go to heaven. Yes, I want to be saved. Yes! I am saved! Glory!" Another trophy to be hung on Sister Lill's wall!

One night during a revival, Sister Lill approached an old country boy named "Bo." Now Bo was country through and through. He would often ride to church on the back of the truck of a Mr. V.S. He had a favorite phrase that preceded anything he would say: "Lord-de-do!" I never knew what that meant, but it must have been important to put into context all that would follow. One night Sister Lill approached Bo during the altar call. Seated on the pew behind Bo, I listened as she started her routine. "Bo, Bo, are you lost?" asked Sister Lill. And Bo, true to form said,

"Lord-de-do, no! I came up here on the back of Mr. V.S.'s truck!"

"All right, Bo! Way to go, Bo!" I whispered under my breath.

Sister Lill turned, face flushed, and walked away as if to say, "Well, go ahead Bo, go to hell if that's your attitude!" She never approached Bo again after that. Bo did not seem to mind at all.

On another night, I remember a man named Will who came to a revival meeting. I had never seen him in church before. He was a friend of mine who also worked for the railroad. (When he retired he gave me a solid bronze switch key that he had used for years in his work, which is still one of my prized treasures.) Now it was said of Will that he drank too much, gambled too much, and cursed too much. Perhaps he did—but there was also a very gentle side of him.

On this particular night, Sister Lill spotted ole Will and sure enough, during the altar call she made a beeline for him, hand on his shoulder, asking the pertinent questions. I watched as ole Will's face turned red in embarrassment and anger! He stepped from his pew, turned and walked straight out the church door. Sister Lill stood there slowly shaking her head. And the congregation continued to sing "Just As I Am" for the third time! Eventually, the service came to a close. Ole Will had escaped the clutches of Sister Lill.

To my knowledge, Will never set foot back in a church again. Within a year, he died. Now it seems to me that since crusaders receive credit for winning people to Christ, it also seems to me that some religious zealots ought to be accountable for turning people away. I don't pretend to know how God felt about Mr. Will and all the "good intentions" of some people, but I like to think He understands. And if God understands, then I think He knows the gentle side of ole Will, the good side that I knew and loved.

And Sister Lill? The last time I saw her in church, she was still doing her thing, the thing that made my blood run cold and put in my mouth a bad taste for fanatical behavior performed in the name of God. About the age of sixteen, I left the church and did not return until I was thirty. Healing takes a long time sometimes.

But, I guess I owe Sister Lill. Years later when I would finish a sermon, and if an invitation was extended, I always hoped and prayed that it was done with grace and dignity and respect for other people's feelings. Disciples are not in the business of trying to scare the hell out of people, but loving heaven *into* them.

Henrietta Keel

Hebrews 11 is a chapter about faith and the faithful. It is a roll call of the heroes of faith. History has recorded many such heroes—Augustine, Polycarp, Luther, St. Francis of Assisi, John and Charles Wesley, and many others too numerous to name. Everybody needs a hero!

In the late 30s and 40s Henrietta Keel would visit the little village of Oakman, Georgia. I was a young boy then, but the image of Henrietta stills remains alive in my memory. For me at this particular time, it was like a miracle; Henrietta Keel came forth from the wilderness in the power of the Spirit. She would visit our church in the summer months, and it was in this setting that she became special in my life.

Henrietta was a rather large woman as I recall. Robust in size and spirit, her presence was almost overpowering. It was during these years that she ministered to people on the streets of Atlanta. She would stand on the street corners and sing spirituals with such a soulful sound that many a human spirit was stirred. Later, she started a mission in what is now known as Cabbage Town.

I was seven years old. She was our Sunday school teacher. She taught us the books of the Bible by singing them to a particular tune. Little did I know the impact that she would have on my life that summer. I remember one night during camp meeting when she stood behind the pulpit in an old tabernacle with the lantern lights dancing all around her. She stood there and began to sing in the raspy, soulful voice that God had given her. It was in these times that I first became aware of God gently drawing me to Himself. If I listen, really listen, I can still hear her singing "Precious Lord, Take My Hand" in her own unique way.

The Grace of God working through Henrietta was a beautiful and gracious thing. She's been in heaven a long time now. I owe her so much. The spirit of Henrietta Keel and the memory of this heroine will live on in my life and the lives of many other people that she touched by her life and testimony.

My dearest Henrietta, "I never thought you'd be my hero. But, you were, and I just want to thank you."

The Old Fisherman

He was sitting on his back porch. It had been raining earlier that day. There was a clean, fresh smell in the air. From the porch, you looked across a pasture, and in the pasture was a barn, on the front of which was a hand painted picture of a mean, raging bull. Looking past the barn, there was a hillside that went up and up, and then, there were only the mountains. Clouds formed and hung low over the mountains. Towering peaks, dark and mysterious, covered with fog and clouds, seemed only a short distance away.

The fisherman was quiet as we sat together on the porch. He was ninety-three years old. Not knowing what to say, I sat in silence with him. He seemed to be lost in his thoughts. And then, suddenly, he leaned forward and pointed his hand toward the mountains and said, "See, it's raining up there on the mountains now."

"Yes Sir," I said. "It looks like it."

And then, there was another pause in the conversation.

"Did you catch any fish today?" he asked.

"No, not many. We caught a few. Nothing of any size though."

"Well they're all cleaned out. Too many fishermen nowadays."

There was another time of silence. I waited for him to continue the dialogue. I knew that he had been a master fly-fisherman in his younger days. So, the next word had to come from him.

Leaning forward in his chair, he said, "When I was a boy and a young man, the fishing was great!" And the stories began.

He recalled the times he had been on the streams at the base of Cold Mountain. There had been numerous success stories of catching trout. As he told the stories, his right hand would be imitating the action of casting a fly line.

He talked about the time he caught a large brown trout at Shining Rock. The hand was in motion. He had made the cast. And, then, suddenly, a large brown trout rose to the fly, the hook was set, and the great brown gave a tremendous fight. My ancient friend described every detail of how he hooked and landed the great fish.

Even though his eyes were age-dimmed, and his steps faltering, his memory was as clear as if it happened yesterday. The stories went on.

I sat and listened with great admiration. As his hand continued to move in the sequence of casting a fly, I looked at the hands. They were wrinkled and the fingers were gnarled. I wondered, *Old hands, how many casts have you made in your lifetime? How many fish have you landed? Did those wild browns give you a great fight?* Then, there was a break in the stories as if he was taking a breather from fishing.

All too soon, it was time to leave. I left him sitting on the porch with the mountains in view. At ninety-three, he lived in another world in another time. As I left, there was a part of me that wished I could have been with him in the time he talked about. It was a time of innocence, when "loyalty" had meaning; a time before cell phones, personal computers, beepers, giant shopping malls, and many other such progressive contrivances.

In a cove in Western North Carolina, the old fisherman sits on his back porch. His eyes are fixed on the mountains in the distance. He remembers the days of long ago and the crystal clear mountain streams. In his memory, the fish are still there in abundance. The cast is made, the fly gently settles on the surface of the water, and he waits . . .

Utility Man

He was always in a hurry. He was the "utility man" in our small town. If you met him on the street, he would be in a dead run—or at least a fast walk that looked like a slow run. "Hey Jack, how's it going?"

"Covered up! I'm totally covered up! Gotta go . . . lots of work . . . just not enough time in the day to get everything done!" This was always his stock-in-trade, answer. And off he would go in a tremendous cloud of dust, sweat, and hypertension.

His utility truck was unlike any other truck that I had ever seen. On board was every conceivable tool and/or piece of machinery. Jack was always prepared! He was ready for a line break, a pole snapping in two, blown transformers and countless other small tragedies. The truck was adorned with a hole digger, extra lengths of power line, fuses, insulated clothing, goggles, a hard hat, hard toe shoes, and a small Gatling gun mounted on the rear just in case! Around his waist he wore a leather belt that was affixed with holsters, clips, and assorted tools and instruments. In the belt were screwdrivers of all kinds and sizes—flatheads, phillips and some that had no name. It also contained pliers, wire cutters, tape, screws, stapler, hammer and various wrenches. When he wore the belt, which was most of the time, he looked like a walking wind chime. Ah, the belt! It was a warrior's belt, the kind of belt that perhaps the god Zeus would have worn. The belt announced who was in charge . . . the utility man of course!

He was always behind schedule because there was never enough time to do such important work. Never enough time! The heavy belt hanging from his waist, pulling down on his utility pants exposed a portion of his anatomy (from the backside) that would have been much better left covered. Somehow, this sight diminished the god Zeus idea. Fast-paced, huffing and puffing, muttering constantly to himself and to those within earshot, "Where has the time gone? Boy, time gets away! Never enough time!"

At thirty-five years of age, we planted Jack in "Rest Haven." He ran out of time. I miss Jack even today. I've often wondered about the belt, the warrior's belt. Does it hang in some attic, collecting dust? Maybe it's stored in some unmarked box never to be bravely worn again.

You don't have to worry anymore about time, old friend, nor do you have to worry about the belt, that heavy warrior's belt, or exposing yourself . . . you are well covered now and for a long, long time.

There is still electricity in the little town, the meters still spin and time goes on.

The Shadow's Voice

Long ago, a youngster walked down a dusty country road on a beautiful day; the sun was bright and the day had just begun. As he walked along, he noticed his distinct shadow. He watched the little puffs of dust his feet made with each step. It had been dry for a long time now. *Maybe* he thought to himself, *it will rain soon and the dust will go away for a while.*

As he continued down the road, he heard an inner voice speaking to him: "C'mon—you think you are really a Christian?"

The boy answered, "Yes, I am a Christian."

"Well if you are, then why did you get mad yesterday with your friend and call him names? Christians don't do that, do they?" the voice asked.

"Uh—well, it was his fault! He started it!"

"So it's O.K. to get mad and call people names if it's their fault? I understand now," the dark voice sneered.

"Oh, by the way," the voice continued, "Christians believe in God, don't they? So tell me, how do you know that God really exists? If you know, prove it to me!" the voice demanded.

"I guess I can't prove it to you, but I know, or, I think I know," the youngster spoke now with less assurance.

Then, another question. "Tell me, young lad, are you afraid to die?"

"Well, I . . . I don't know," the boy barely spoke the words.

"But I know! I know! You are afraid! It would be the end of you!" said the taunting, shadowy voice.

Suddenly, the sun went behind the clouds. The boy noticed that his shadow, which was so pronounced a minute ago, had now completely disappeared. Mysteriously, the voice was silent. A cool breeze began to blow. The clouds grew darker. In the distant hills he could see heavy rain falling, moving toward him. The boy found shelter and sat quietly as the rain fell and refreshed the earth.

The rain made everything smell fresh and new. Then, he heard another voice from within. This time the voice was calm. It was like a still, small voice of assurance. "Do not be afraid. I love you and I will always be with you." And from the boy's spirit sprang forth the familiar words, "Jesus loves me, this I know, for the Bible tells me so."

Years have passed since that time. Now an old man, he realizes that there is within us a dark side. It is the shadowy side of our nature. When it speaks, it introduces doubt, confusion, fear, and unrest.

Over the years, he has learned that there is a Spirit that has the power to silence the shadowy voice of darkness—the Spirit of Christ Himself.

Bad-Eye and a Boy

It was a hot summer night in August. The light coming from the kerosene lanterns mounted on the walls of the sanctuary gave off a dancing, flickering flame, and provided an eerie feeling to a young boy sitting in the rough-slatted pews. It was hot, and the youngster was tired. The preacher had been preaching for more than an hour! The young boy's mind and the part of his anatomy designed for sitting had just about had all he could stand for one night.

The preacher was now hoarse, but he still displayed much vigor and energy. The necktie had long since been loosened so he could breathe more air. Shirt wringing wet with sweat, handkerchief in hand to mop his brow and the corners of his mouth, he preached, and preached, and preached . . .

"I tell you hell is waiting! Listen to me, sinners! God's gonna clean up this world! The flames of hell are hot! Sinners will go there and burn forever! Bootleggers, whiskey runners, gamblers, whore chasers, and drunkards will split hell wide open!" (It was said of Bad-Eye that he had majored in all of the above.) "Men like Bad-Eye Dalton will be found there screaming and crying for release from the tormenting flames! Indeed! God is going to rid the world of the scum of the earth! Amen?"

And the congregation shouted, "Amen!"

The young boy wondered what God thought about that . . . *Oh, no, there goes Bad-Eye Dalton. He was con-*

signed to hell by a Fundamentalist, sweating, shouting, pulpit-pounding preacher.

The boy didn't sleep much that night. Thoughts of flames, scorching flesh, and Bad-Eye Dalton filled his young mind. A guilty feeling swept over him because he could not say with the congregation "Amen" when the preacher consigned Bad-Eye to hell. Actually, he liked Bad-Eye for reasons he did not understand at the time.

Oakman, Georgia was a small community in the foothills of the Blue Ridge Mountains. The small town consisted of several homes, a gas station, post office, grocery store, a blacksmith shop, and Bad-Eye Dalton and his followers.

The filling station (service station in this modern era) was the place where Bad-Eye and his band of merry men would congregate on the weekend. It was their sanctuary. The boy lived next door. Many times he had been warned by his mother never to hang out at the filling station with these low-life vermin!

Saturday was their usual day of meeting. The only thing that separated the boy's home from the station was a narrow driveway and a grease rack used for changing oil and maintenance of cars. However, on most occasions, this particular spot formed the text for the preacher's sermon the following Sunday.

One Saturday, the boy saw Bad-Eye backing his old car up in front of the grease rack. He watched as Bad-Eye got out of his car and walked slowly around to the front. He stood there silently surveying the surroundings.

Bad-Eye wore a black patch over his left eye. His hair was a gray-yellow color, pasted down with Vitalis hair tonic. (The dry look had not yet evolved.) He was not a slave to dress. His clothes were always wrinkled and dirty from too much wear and not enough wash. His index and middle finger on his left hand were stained dark yellow from the cigarettes that he chain smoked. Phillip Morris was his master and he yielded graciously. His voice had a husky quality which the boy assumed was derived from all those cigarettes combined with too much corn whiskey.

Bad-Eye drove an old Model A Ford that spit and sputtered, clinked and clunked its way to the grease rack meeting. Bad-Eye—High priest of the grease rack church.

To the religious community, Bad-Eye was a thorn in the flesh. No one knew what to do about him. If they had known, it would not have mattered because legend had it that Bad-Eye was a mean son-of-a-bitch who did what he wanted to do. He was his own man. Thus, judgment and condemnation to hell without one ounce of grace was awarded to him.

He could hold the attention of the members of his "church of the grease rack" with his storytelling. Bad-Eye, with his switchblade knife, cleaning his fingernails while smoking a cigarette, could weave a story that would make your blood run cold. It was rumored that he had done much damage with his switchblade on more than one occasion to some unfortunate soul who had crossed him.

It was one fine Saturday morning when the boy slipped away from home and went down to the filling station. Some of the grease rack congregation had already started assembling. About the time the boy got there, Bad-Eye drove up and backed his car in front of the grease rack. As was his custom, he opened the door of his car and stepped out slowly, observing who was present for the meeting. The black patch looked even more awesome to the boy. Bad-Eye then leaned into the car and pulled out a gallon jug of something liquid and placed it on the front fender of his car. The boy surmised that it was not communion wine. The motor of the car was still running. *Chug, chug, chug.* The little engine sang the anthem of Bad-Eye.

"Hey, get a glass, fellers!" he said in his husky voice. Quickly from within the station, glasses and cups were retrieved. Bad-Eye began to pour from the gallon jug. "Here, drink up," he said as the cups and glasses were filled. "Best batch I've made!"

Bad-Eye sat on the fender next to the jug, cigarette dangling between his yellowed fingers, a glass of moonshine in his right hand, and his stories began. There were stories of bloody fights interrupted by "Here, fill that glass again!" and he continued.

There were stories of being chased by the county sheriff. "Have another round!" There were stories of women he had pursued, women who had fallen in love with him. "Here, give me that cup, you need a refill . . . yes, sir!" There were stories of whiskey making and whiskey running. He hauled his own from the woods to the intended destination. And, there were stories of pulpit pounders who were secret customers of his. And the congregation was greatly amused.

Another full jug was produced from the back of his car. Motor still running, whiskey jug on the fender, tale after tale was spun from the archives of Bad-Eye's memory. Soon, Bad-Eye and his followers were well on the way to being full of the spirit. (The kind that comes in a bottle or jug.) There was much laughter and loud talking. Eventually, someone stumbled and fell against the front fender on which the moonshine rested. The gallon jug was knocked over and the explosive contents spilled into the running engine of Bad-Eye's pride and joy. *"Chug, chug, chug-a-lug . . . "*

Needless to say, there was no small explosion! The congregation scattered! They were hoping for a speedy benediction, but it did not come. Bad-Eye stepped back as he watched the flames shoot out from the motor and in quick work engulf the car. His eyes were filled with rage!

"Whoa, stop! Get back! Stop! Stop, you flames!" as though even the flames could understand him. Finally, he realized it was useless. He took a few more steps backward. "All right, all right!" he shouted. "Burn, you bastard! Burn you sonja-bitch! Go on, go on, burn yourself straight to hell!"

Bad-Eye had a way with words.

The boy watched and remembered the pounding pulpit preacher who had so often consigned Bad-Eye and men like him to hell! And now, the High Priest of the Grease Rack Church was consigning his own car to the pit of hell!

The boy wondered what God thought about that . . .

After the eternal consignment, Bad-Eye lit another cigarette, took a long drink from the glass he was holding and broke out into a gut-bursting laugh. The old Ford had been totally consumed by the flames. Jugs exploding from the rear seat had helped the meeting come to a close.

"Amen."

After that day, Bad-Eye was seen no more. Some people say he took the bus out of town the next day. Others claim he met a tragic end in a knife fight in another town. Whatever his fate, Bad-Eye was never seen again in Oakman, Georgia

His congregation scattered. The grease rack at the filling station seemed empty now, especially on weekends.

The Baptist Church? It's still there to this very day. The parishioners have gone back to their worship and no doubt are convinced that God did his job and did it well. And the preacher is looking for a new text.

The young boy? Well he's now a grown man and a preacher himself. But he remembers Bad-Eye and all the times that he had been consigned to hell. Even while preaching, there were times when his thoughts traveled back to Bad-Eye Dalton. Somewhere, deep inside his soul, he wishes that Bad-Eye would walk through the double doors and sit down in the sanctuary on any given Sunday. If it were to happen and even if he were in the process of preaching a sermon, he knows he would stop and slowly walk up to where Bad-Eye is seated. He would look him in the eye and say, "Bad-Eye, it's good to see you. I'm glad you came here today. You are always welcome here." There would be no sharp tones of judgment or condemnation, but the preacher would do his best to offer grace, forgiveness, and acceptance.

"And, by the way, Bad-Eye, where in hell have you been?"

The Waitress

(Or, learning new pronouns)

It had been a long, hard day of fishing in the mountains. The weather was hot and very humid. Tired, hungry, and thirsty, we came to a small town and looked for a restaurant. We finally found one that looked good, mainly because it was still open. So, we went in and were seated. The restaurant was almost empty with the exception of two other customers.

Finally, a waitress came over to our table. "What can I get yo'uns to drink?" she asked. I looked at my fishing partner and waited for his reply. However, before he could answer, she continued. "Yo'uns ought not to drink the tea, sweetened or unsweetened." We had to ask why, but I wish we had not.

"Why?" my partner asked.

"Because," said she, "them guys in the back stir it with their whole arm down in the tea." She was telling me more than I wanted to know. "Are cokes already mixed?" I asked!

She laughed. "Why, yes they are, silly!" We ordered cokes.

"Oh! Yo'uns ought not eat the onion rings either."

My partner just had to ask, "Why not?"

"Because them onions rings are nasty!" Well, at least the menu was being narrowed down. For some reason, my appetite was diminishing.

The waitress leaned over our table as if to divulge a

deep, dark secret. Her voice was little more than a whisper. "Yo'uns see them guys sitting over there?" as she slightly nodded her head in their direction.

How could we miss them? We were seated next to them.

"Well," she said, "yo'uns might ought to move; them guys are weird!" So we moved over two tables farther away.

Appetite further diminished. Eventually, we ordered some fish that we hoped was safe to eat. We were almost through eating when the two "weird" guys left. Immediately, the waitress came over and asked us a penetrating question: "Did yo'uns smell them boys when they left? They smelt bad!"

I was now through eating my meal. "Oh, by the way, are yo'uns seniors?"

I was afraid to say anything. "If yo'uns are, tell that woman over there by the cash register and she will give you ten percent off this bill." By now I felt they should have paid us to eat there.

Before we could get up from the table, she was back again. "I thought yo'uns might want a toothpick." With that, she placed a toothpick by each plate.

We'uns came, we'uns ate, and we'uns left. We'uns even left a tip because we'uns were grateful that we'uns had survived a traumatic ordeal. And, we'uns had learned some new pronouns from a well-meaning waitress.

The Hunter

My father was a hunter. There was an earthiness about him that I liked even though at the time I did not know what to name it. He knew about trees, stars, and much of what belongs to the Created Order. As for his formal education, I think he finished the seventh grade. But that was another time, another era. In his own way, he was a man of great knowledge, understanding, and he had an extraordinary appreciation of nature. He loved the smell of newly turned earth; he loved summer rains, especially when the earth was dry and the raindrops pelted the land kicking up tiny dust balls. "Frogs," that's what he called them.

We hunted together. In those days, there were no deer to hunt, so most of the hunting consisted of coon, rabbit, squirrel, and turkey. He had a great respect for wildlife. Never did we kill anything except for eating purposes. In our home, there was no such thing as "trophy" hunting.

My father had two coon dogs, "Blue" and "Brownie." He was never given to creative naming of the hounds. He had scraped together enough money to buy the pups, and he had trained them until they were able to track and tree a coon almost without fail. Life was not easy; but through it all, he valued the small, simple things that enriched our existence.

I treasure each memory of the hunts we had together. Our favorite hunting place was in the area of Sleuder

Mountain. Most of the coon hunts were in the dead of winter. In those days insulated hunting clothes were an unknown. We made do with what we had.

I still remember the smell of the fumes of the kerosene lantern as we made our way through the woods in the darkness of night. We traveled light in the North Georgia Mountains. We would take a few sandwiches, an ax, a lantern, and a large tin can in which coffee would be made at some point during the hunt.

I recall crossing streams frozen solid from the harsh breath of winter. During the hunt we would always take a break. While my father built a fire, I would break the ice in the stream and fill the can with water. We would dump coffee into the can of water and let it boil. It contained a few grounds to be sure, but it was some of the best coffee in the world! We would rest while the coffee was boiling and listen to the dogs bark as they trailed a coon.

"Hey, listen to old Blue," Dad would say. "He's hot on the trail! Won't be long now. Soon they'll have that coon up a tree!" He could tell by the bark of the dogs whether or not they had treed the coon.

Those nights in the woods were like magic. Sipping our coffee and listening to the voices of the dogs, my dad seemed to be relaxed and at peace with the young boy's wonderful world. Sitting under the canopy of heaven, warmed by the fire, there was little need for spoken words. Stars, million of stars twinkled in rhythm to the crackling of the fire and the lonesome sound of Blue and Brownie calling out to us.

It was on Sleuder Mountain that my father showed me my first deer track. Deer had been scarce for years, but now he hoped they were making a comeback. It was at the base of Sleuder Mountain that he told me of the wild horses he had seen as a young boy. They would graze in the apple orchards. Wild horses! They had never been tamed nor would they ever be tamed . . . but now, they were no more. I watched and listened as he spoke of the past. His steely blue eyes were alive with excitement as he recalled those memories of long ago.

I remember he spoke to me once about the mystery of sound. "You know," he said, "when the wind blows through the trees and there's nothing else to catch your attention, it's as though you can hear the voice of God." He believed that in it all and through it all, God was present. Now my father was not a religious man in the sense of organized religion, but in the depth of his soul, he knew that here in this setting, God was.

My father was a man of few words. He didn't often speak of inner feelings. Maybe they were too deep for him to try to verbalize. It could have been that he was afraid of being embarrassed if he spoke words like, "I love you." Whatever the reasons in the early years, he seldom expressed his emotions. However, I learned that love and compassion were spoken in other ways.

It was the first hunt with my father that this discovery was made.

One day he came in from work after a week on the road driving one of the "big rigs." It was the first time he ever asked me if I wanted to go on a hunt with him. I was only about ten or twelve years old.

"You want to go squirrel hunting in the morning?" he asked. It was unbelievable!

Me? Really hunting with my dad?

"Yes," I shouted, "I sure do."

My mother was not too thrilled with this. She thought I was much too young to go hunting, but my dad won the debate. So early next morning, we took the old "handmade," flat-bottom river boat to the Coosawattee

River and put in just about daylight. Arrangements were made for us to be picked up miles downriver late that afternoon.

We got in the boat. I sat up front and my dad was in the back to paddle and guide the boat. He handed me his double barrel, twelve-gauge shotgun along with several boxes of shells. He instructed me on how to shoot squirrels in this kind of hunting. We floated down the river from daylight to almost dark. I spent the entire day shooting squirrels. I must have shot at least four boxes of shells. To this day, it remains one of the greatest hunts of my life.

At the end of the hunt, dad guided the boat into a landing area where we were to be picked up. The boat was full of squirrels—enough in fact to feed several families in Oakman, Georgia. As he rowed the boat over to the bank, I jumped out and, taking the rope tied to the front of the boat, pulled it up as far as I could on the sandbar.

Feelings of great exhilaration filled my young spirit. What a day! What a hunt! Holding the boat steady as my father got out, I noticed for the first time how tired he really was. It was then that I saw his hands. Tough hands he had. But the palms of those tough, calloused hands were covered with blood. The blisters that had burst from rowing the boat with a crude paddle were oozing blood. My father had not taken a shot all day. This day, this hunt had been a gift to me. He did not have to say, "I love you." The sight of his hands pierced my heart. The bleeding hands and a father's love are well-secured in the archives of my memory.

Then came the day when "Ole Blue" was taken ill. The vet said he had cancer and there was nothing he could do. The vet asked my father, "Do you want me to put him to sleep?"

"No," my father replied. "Give me what I need and I will take it home and do it myself " I knew my father was hurting because he loved that hound so much! I wished there was something I could do.

When we arrived home, my father took Blue along with the lethal injection to the dog pen. It seemed like an eternity before he came back into the house. He stood silently for a time in the kitchen. Then he said, "I can't do it. You'll have to do it for me and Blue." He handed me the injection. That day remains vivid in my mind. I walked out to the dog pen. Blue was lying on the ground barely moving. His sad eyes opened and closed slowly.

"Blue, so many good times we've enjoyed together. Why did this have to happen to you?" I asked as if Blue understood. Perhaps he did.

Slowly I injected the needle into Blue's hip. I waited. In a few moments, his breathing stopped and his eyes closed for the last time. I went back into the house to tell my father that Blue was gone.

Slowly, my father got out of his chair. "Do you want me to help you?" I asked. "No," he said, "I will bury him myself." He walked out to the dog pen. I knew he wanted to be alone. I guess there are some things you need to do by yourself. From the window of the kitchen, I watched his helplessness as he cradled Blue in his arms and made his way from the pen toward the woods. To this day, I don't know where he buried "ole Blue." When he returned from the burial, I saw the pain in my father's eyes. We never spoke of the incident again.

Years have passed since then, and now, my father is gone. We buried him on my birthday. Three months later, my mother died. Two of the most important people in my life are now gone. Not a young man anymore myself, I no longer hunt, but most of my time is spent in the mountains fly-fishing. When I am alone fishing for trout in some remote mountain stream, I often remember those days of a father's love and compassion. Even now, the voice of God can still be heard in the wind as it gently blows through the trees, or in the sound of the river as it flows over the rocks. It is during these times that I often recall my father and the simplicity of his life.

Ah, the mountains, those haunting mountains, where even now, if I listen carefully, I can still hear the baying hounds and smell the brewing coffee on a cold, winter night long ago.

The Mourning Tree

Through the rock-wall gate there is a road,
A narrow, winding road that leads to a
    place, a resting place.
Along the road on both sides are old trees,
    overlapping, heavy with years, tired and sad.
And why not? They've seen much sorrow.

With the passing years caravans of hearts
    heavy with grief, traveled this path.
The old trees have seen many tears.
They have heard deep mourning of love
    now gone.
They've watched people embrace each other
    for support.

The old trees have heard the readings, the prayers
    and meaningless words spoken.
They've watched people come to this place
    and stare in disbelief.
They've seen the hole in the ground waiting to be
    filled with a body.
And when the wind blows softly, they can be heard
    weeping.

"Amen." And the people rise slowly to leave,
    feet heavy, bodies weary.
And the procession goes out the way it came in.
It has been completed, finished. Everyone has
    gone.
But the trees remain, watching over
    what has been done.

Papa

Papa was a man of few words. Actually, he was our grandpa, but we all called him "Papa." He was no stranger to hard work. Whatever education he had was mostly from the "school of hard knocks."

Each summer when school was out, I worked for him. He had a corn-shelling business and a corn mill. I vividly recall how hot it was in those old farm corncribs! Shoveling corn all day was not much fun. I never thought it built character.

I watched Papa year after year. He had always seemed old. Early on in my life, I determined that I did not want to be like him. No, sir! Enough of this backbreaking hard work! There had to be more to life than this!

Well, Papa has been gone a long time. Many changes have taken place since his exodus. But, I still remember . . .

In my imagination I can see him—an old man, sitting under a giant oak shade tree eating his lunch that he carried in an old beat-up black lunchbox. The shade tree was his temporary sanctuary where he found relief from the scorching heat of a hot July day.

Sometimes Papa would take a nap during the lunch break. Usually though, he would sit on the ground and lean back against the tree with his soiled hat pulled down over his eyes. Lunch break was for eating and resting and it always took exactly sixty minutes, no more, no less! Papa carried a Hamilton pocket watch tethered to the bib of his overalls by a frayed shoestring. When he reached for the watch you knew it was time to go back to work.

Papa was one of the most patient men I have ever known. The corn sheller was old and worn out. It would often break down. I remember many times when Papa would spend hours in the scorching summer heat working on it. Never once did I see him lose his patience or become visibly upset. As soon as it was fixed he would call out to us, "Okay, back to work, boys!"

One day after work as we were driving home, he pulled the loaded truck into a secluded spot alongside Talking Rock Creek. I was lying in the bed of the truck that was filled with shelled corn. I leaned over the top of the sideboards and watched him get out of the truck. Before I realized what he was doing, Papa was "skinny-dipping" in the creek. When he dived into the water, he stayed under for a long time. I remember thinking, *That old man is much too old for this kind of behavior. He's probably drowned!* Finally, he surfaced and I heard him holler "Wheeeooow! Water's cold! C'mon in!"

Papa was a religious man. I watched him in church. Music touched his heart and soul. Anytime "Amazing Grace" was sung, it was as though the old man had been on the Mount of Transfiguration! You could see the transformation in his face.

There were quiet times . . . I've seen tears run down his face as he was "moved by the Spirit." No words had to be spoken in order to understand what was happening. It was told to me that when a grandson was born, Papa spoke a word of prophecy concerning the child and his vocation. Something about being a preacher I think.

Any changes since the old man made his departure from this world? Yes. One that comes to mind is—I wish I were more like Papa.

High-Tech Friend

I admit it. I am not a "high-tech" person. I can turn my computer on and off, I can use the word processor; I can manage to get online on the Internet, and that's about it. Our VCR still blinks 12:00 all the time. I do not have a clue on how to set the thing. We bought an electric alarm clock (digital!) and it took a couple of weeks to set it correctly. The alarm button and snooze button were not clearly defined in the little manual that I did not read until weeks later. Well, you get the picture. I'm not high tech, but I have a friend . . .

Compared to my friend, I should be given a degree from Georgia Tech in "advanced technology"! He is brilliant. In many fields he is an expert. He is well traveled. He can speak on almost any subject with great knowledge and authority. He has a great personality. He has a story available for any event that will always bring forth laughter. He is a true friend and fishing partner. But, I must be truthful here. When it comes to living in the high-tech world, he is lacking—and that is a tremendous understatement.

You know the cordless phones that allow you to go from room to room and carry on a conversation when someone calls you? My friend has one of those. One day on a fishing trip, he was found to be high atop Buford Dam on the Chattahoochee River with his cordless phone in hand, dialing his home number. Again and again he dialed the number. Finally hitting the "off button" on the cordless home phone, he was heard muttering something like "Hummph! This high tech stuff never works when you need it!"

There was the time when he was sitting in his recliner at home watching TV. He is an ardent fan of old western movies. The phone rang and his wife answered it. She said to him, "Honey, pick up the phone. It's for you."

So, he reached for the cordless phone but instead picked up the remote control for the TV. "Hello, hello, hello! Well speak up if you are there!" There was a note of irritation in his voice. Then he said to his wife, "Hon, there's not anyone on the phone," as he placed the remote down and continued to watch *Bad Men of Tombstone.*

And there came the day when he needed to page his wife at work. So, he dialed her page number. When the phone gave the busy signal indicating that now is the time to enter your number, he entered his number in his own unique way. When his wife came home, she asked him, "Did you try to page me today?"

"Yes I did, but you didn't answer your page," he said.

"But you didn't enter your number!" she responded.

"I did so!" he said, with a slightly raised voice. He continued to explain, "When I heard the busy signal, I spoke my number into the phone and then I hit the pound button." Shaking his head in frustration, he said, "I tell you hon, this high-tech stuff just doesn't work very well!"

Perhaps that's one of the reasons we are friends. When it comes to the high-tech stuff, we both stand on the brink of illiteracy.

But, you know what? That's O.K.

Obe

It was a bitter cold winter morning. The wind cut like a knife through my heavy coat. As I was leaving the post office I saw him. He was standing across the street wearing his familiar tattered hat and long, oversized coat that hung from his slender shoulders giving the appearance that he was carrying the weight of the world on his back. He was old and had to walk with a cane. His skin looked like leather from having been exposed to the summer's sun and the winter's cold. His face was marked with deep lines of age. Always, you could see snuff around the corners of his mouth. That was Obe ... old Obe, the town bum.

I walked across the street and spoke to him. As usual, he hit me up for a couple of dollars promising to pay me back next week. I knew and he knew that next week would not bring him any more money than he had this week. But it was O.K.

He looked very tired on this cold morning.

"Obe, how are you doing?" I asked.

"I don't feel good today," he replied.

"Well, come on, Obe. I'll walk home with you."

"Thank you. I appreciate it," he said.

It was some home! He lived in an old run-down house owned by the United Methodist Church. Soon, it was to be torn down to make room for an additional parking lot. Obe lived in one room of the big house. We entered the room and Obe removed his coat, throwing it over the chair by his bed. A single light bulb at the end of a cord hung from the ceiling giving off very little light. The room was cold. Obe walked over to the unvented gas heater and turned it up as high as it would go.

"Sit down and stay awhile," he said as he began to warm some coffee on a hot plate.

"O.K., I'll stay a few minutes. Obe, you know I've never been in your home before."

"I know." Something about the way he said that made me feel uncomfortable. I guess he expected a visit every now and then from the minister. I thought, *He's not a member; so don't worry about it. After all, I have given him a few dollars in the past.* Somehow this exercise in rationalization did not make me feel any better!

Obe sat down on the edge of his bed. He removed his hat and hung it on the bedpost. A few strands of dirty, gray hair fell across his forehead as he shook his head from side to side.

"Boy, I really feel bad. Don't know what it is. Oh well, I guess it will pass."

"Obe, is there anything I can do for you?" I asked.

"No, no, I don't know of anything. You can stay for a while if you have time." It was an invitation that could not be turned down.

The folks in town never gave Obe much attention. After all, he was uneducated and had no visible means of support, so how could he be of any help to the community? Obe was just a town fixture that people had grown accustomed to seeing . . . and that was all.

We sat in his one room for what seemed like minutes before he spoke again. I was seeing Obe for the first time in a different light. He was just like everyone else— except he had less. I had never heard Obe talk much, but on that day, he began telling me something about himself.

He talked about his boyhood days. His daddy had been a sharecropper. He talked about the times he followed his daddy as he plowed the fields. He liked the smell of freshly turned earth. He spoke of summer rain after a long drought, and how good it was. He said the summer rain brought with it freshness. It had a clean smell and made everything seem new. For the first time, I noticed a peaceful look on Obe's face. With a twinkle in his eye, he talked about "skinny-dipping" in the creek down in the bottoms. And the fish? Well, you wouldn't believe the size of some of the fish he used to catch. Life had been hard for Obe, but he still had some good memories.

Suddenly his mood changed. He became quiet for a few moments, and then he began another story. "There was this girl named Jenny," he said. "She had golden hair and her eyes were the bluest I'd ever seen. She was so pretty. She was the daughter of the landowner. She was always real nice to me. She was a special young lady. Her folks didn't want her to have anything to do with the likes of me. You know, I really loved Jenny. She was the only one in my whole life." Obe withdrew into silence.

I sat there for a short time thinking that he might want to talk some more. But he didn't. He just sat on the edge of his bed as if I were not there.

"Obe, I have to go. I guess I'll see you later," I said as I got up to leave. He stared silently into the yesterdays of his life. He did not acknowledge my leaving. I guess I was surprised that Obe had feelings like everyone else. He had experienced life and hard times. But he loved, and he had remembered.

Two days later, Obe was found lying on his bed . . . dead. The little gas heater was still burning high. The coffee pot remained on the hot plate. His overcoat was drooped over the chair where he had left it and his old tattered hat was still hanging on the bedpost. Nothing had been changed since the day I was with him . . . except now, he was dead.

Obe, I wish I had done more for you. The memory of your meager existence still haunts me to this day. I am thankful that you shared some of your story with me, especially about Jenny. Thanks for teaching me a lesson about reaching out to others who really need us. Obe, I hope you can forgive me.

The town paid his funeral expenses.The suit he was buried in cost more than any clothes he ever wore when he was alive.

Obe died in abject poverty next door to a church that had plenty. And I . . . I was the pastor of that church.

Dora

If you travel north on Highway 441, you will pass a house on the right before you get to Cornelia, Georgia. It's an old house. Weather-beaten and dilapidated, it stands as a monument to the past. On one side of the house is a small porch and on the porch sits an over-sized stuffed chair. It, too, reflects the many years of us-age. Some of the chair's stuffing protrudes from the arms and back.

If you should happen to drive by in warm weather, you will probably see a woman sitting in the chair watch-ing traffic go by. Her name is Dora (pronounced Do'ree). Like the house and the chair, Dora's appearance reflects years of living. Her hair is white and unruly strands can sometimes be seen dangling from under a knit cap. Her skin is wrinkled and her complexion tells you that she has seen many days in the sun. Even in warm weather, she wears a sweater that is tattered and torn, much like the chair. Her bony hand and fingers are constantly tug-ging and smoothing her hair. One day while driving by, my wife and I saw her on the porch. Luckily, I had my camera with me. The weathered house, the raggedy stuffed chair, and Dora would make a great picture. We stopped, got out of the car and walked up to the porch. After introducing ourselves, I asked if I could take her picture.

"But I'm not fixed up," she said as she ran her fingers

through her hair and pulled at her sweater.

"You're fine. You look just fine," we assured her.

"Well, if you think so. I guess it's all right," she replied.

"I tell you what I'll do. I will make some pictures of you and send you copies. Will that be O.K.?"

"Well, all right. But I wish I was fixed up better." She was still tugging at her sweater and hair.

That day I shot a roll of film of the house and Dora. All the time we were there, she was talking. We assumed she had few visitors. In about thirty minutes, we learned some of her history. She had lived alone for several years following the death of her husband.

"You know, in a few months I will be ninety years old! What do you think about that?" She was very proud of her age.

"Dora, I think that is great." It was almost Thanksgiving and I wondered how or if she would celebrate Thanksgiving Day.

"What are you going to do on Thanksgiving?" I asked.

"Oh, nothing, I guess. It's just another day for me. I'm almost ninety, you know. Most of my friends are gone. I still have a son who lives in Cornelia, Georgia. He may come by for a while." She continued to tell us about her past and some of her experiences. She was born in the house where she now lives. In all her years, this had been her only home.

As we prepared to leave, she was still talking. About halfway to the car, she called out to us. We turned to view this petite woman who looked so small sitting in the over-sized chair. Then she said once again, "You know in a few months I will be ninety years old. And listen, I want you to know that I love you!" Ah, small woman, such big words!

Since then, I've often thought of her. The cool weather has probably driven her inside. I wonder what she does all day? Does she have enough to eat? Will she be able to stay warm in that big house?

When we left her that day, our hearts were warmed by her friendliness and her excitement about an upcoming birthday. To be almost ninety and still have a twinkle in the eye is truly a gift of God.

Happy Thanksgiving and happy birthday, Dora. We love you too.

Reasons to Be Thankful

Before the great rivers,
   And the majestic mountains,
   And the canyons came into being
God was.

Between "In the Beginning . . ."
   And "Come Lord Jesus,
   An unfolding story took center stage,
And the Alpha and Omega was.

Before you were born,
   And before I was born,
   And time was set in motion,
The Creator had a plan.

When darkness covered the deep,
   And earth was a formless void,
   And the waters were swept with wind,
The Creator God thought.

The existing thoughts of God
   Were put into words,
   And the words called into being,
Created light to a darkened world.

Then dust of the ground and bone of bone,
   And flesh of flesh,
   And man and woman came into being,
Male and female—and love existed.

God's thoughts became words,

And the Word became flesh,
And we beheld His glory,
And Jesus was.

A babe in a manger, a boy in the Temple,
A Savior on the Cross,
A Risen Christ from the tomb of death,
And Agape produced Salvation.

The Creator God lives!
The Son of God lives!
His Spirit lives today!
And because He lives, we will live also!

Old Preacher Man

When I walked into ICU, I wasn't sure if it was you or not. You looked different. For one thing, your hair was all messed up. And all those tubes changed the way you looked. You scared me. I had to look twice just to make sure it was you. The furrowed brow, the swollen, blood-shot eyes and three-day-old beard, coupled with your labored breathing, projected a picture of helplessness . . . and that's scary, old man, it's really scary!

As I stood by your bed, I didn't know if you knew me. You tried to talk but I couldn't understand you. There was a terrible rattling sound in your lungs as you breathed. I remembered long ago, how folks would talk about the sound of the "death rattle" that occurs to people shortly before they die. I wanted to do something but there was nothing I could do. I prayed for you.

I recall just a few weeks ago, we were on a district ministers' retreat together. You were always in charge of making the coffee. We had a ritual, remember? I would get a cup of coffee and then tell you how bad it was. And you would always respond with—"If you don't like my coffee make it yourself!"

Then, there was the golf ritual. "When are we going to play golf?" you would ask.

"I don't know," I would answer . . . "Perhaps next month?" And we both knew that we would not play next month or even next year. I don't know how all that got started.

In those few minutes as I watched you, I knew that it could be me lying there instead of you. No one is exempt from sickness and suffering and death! No one! I thought, *What would I do if I were in that bed? How could I provide for my family? Where would my wife live? What would I be without her, a church, a people, and a sermon?*

Well, old man, I must tell you! Because of you, I didn't sleep much last night. I kept seeing you again and again in my mind. I saw the pain, the fear, and the hurt and frustration. You kept me awake most of the night. And deep down inside of me where fear rises now and then, were thoughts of you. My heart went out to you. You were in my thoughts and prayers.

It's daylight now. I look out the window and a new day is beginning. The grass is so green, the plumes in the island are gently blowing in the morning breeze, and I'm lying in my bed next to the woman I love. It doesn't get much better than this!

As far as I know, I'm in good health. I realize that I have wasted much of the night worrying about what could be rather than what is. So I have to ask myself, "What am I going to do with this day?"

For starters, I'm going to tell my wife how much I love her and how I want to spend the rest of my life with her. I'm going to get up and be about ministry, whenever and wherever the opportunity presents itself, and I'm going to make the most of this day that I possibly can.

Get well, old preacher man . . . there's much life yet to be lived!

Virgie McKinzey

As I entered her room, I knew the end was near. Her breathing was labored, and she did not respond at all to my voice or when I touched her hand. She had been a friend for so long. It was hard to believe that she would soon be leaving.

On the wall at the head of her bed were a couple of framed articles that I had written long ago. One of the articles was about her and her own brand of uniqueness. Virgie was "one-of-a-kind." She was ninety years old and the curtain of her life was slowly being lowered.

On the nightstand next to her bed were some pictures. One of the frames held two small pictures. On one side was a handsome young sailor. On the other, there was a beautiful seventeen-year-old girl with a smile that spoke of love and excitement about the future. I looked at the pictures and was reminded of the story behind them. The young sailor and the beautiful seventeen-year-old girl were going to be married. But the young man was killed in an automobile accident. I don't know if Virgie ever dated anyone after that, but she never married.

Standing next to her bed, my mind raced back to our first encounter, which was somewhat less than good. Actually, it was a terrible beginning, but regardless—or maybe because of it—we became the best of friends.

One Sunday morning in church, Virgie got up out of her seat and walked down the aisle as we were singing the closing hymn. I held my breath as she slowly made her way to the altar with the help of her ever-present cane. One could never be sure what Virgie would do! Then she asked, "You got any water in that bowl, Rev?" (She was referring to the baptismal font.)

"No, Virgie, I don't."

"Well get some then!" she replied. "I want to be baptized and join this church!"

"Well, all right Virgie!" I said.

We stopped everything, fetched some water and baptized her that day. Ah, that was a very good thing!

When I turned forty years old, she surprised me with a birthday party at a restaurant in Athens, Georgia. Many people from the church were present. As we ate dinner, I detected the sound of distant drums that grew louder with each passing second. A curtain on a small stage parted, and a belly dancer emerged doing her thing (and did it very well as I recall). It was a memorable evening.

While I was recovering from surgery at Emory Hospital, I received a gift of some beautiful artificial flowers, contained in a shiny new urinal. Virgie had wished me well.

A day came when Virgie asked me, "Rev, what are you going to say at my funeral?"

"I don't know," I said. "I will try to think of something nice."

Her response was "Hell, Rev, tell it like it is, just tell it like it is!"

There was no pretense with Virgie; she was a warm and earthy person who did not have a dishonest bone in her body. I'm sure she shocked some people by statements she made on many occasions, but that was Virgie! I loved her straightforward way of speaking, and I respected her because you never had to wonder what she was thinking . . . she enjoyed telling you!

Before I left her room that night, I leaned over her bed and prayed for her. Then I whispered, "Good-bye, old friend." There was no response. The next morning at 4:05 A.M. she died.

At the graveside, I did my best to honor her request to "Tell it like it is, Rev, just tell it like it is!"

She was one of a kind.

Mr. Flemming: The Dreamer

Dreams are a must if we are to live life to its fullest. I'm not talking about the dreams we have when we sleep, but dreams that we have within. A goal in life could be a dream. Dreams are made of substances that motivate, energize, and sustain us in difficult times. Many biblical and historical figures have been great dreamers. Some dreams may never reach fruition, but as long as they are alive, hope is alive, and hope enriches the life we live.

I met Mr. Fleming years ago. His days were filled with time spent sitting in the dining hall and the hallways of the convalescent home. His physical body was feeble, but his mind was sharp and alert. His eyes were as blue as the sky, and you could see in them that he had a dream or two that were still alive.

He spent his days among people not all of whom communicated very well. Many of them were strapped in their chairs staring expressionlessly ahead. One lady repeated certain sentences over and over all day long. Another man made repetitive movements or gestures that he repeated continuously. An elderly lady sat in her chair softly humming old familiar tunes she had learned from childhood.

And across the room, the old man sat alone with his thoughts. After visiting some people I knew, I walked over to the old man and spoke to him. He invited me to take a seat next to him. He considered himself an artist and poet. He gave me a large picture of a horse he had drawn. It was not a well-proportioned picture of a horse, but it was his horse and for him it was perfect. On the back of the picture he had written a short poem about the horse:

> Roses are red,
> Violets are blue,
> Racehorses that lose,
> Are turned into glue!

When I looked at him after reading the poem, those steel-blue eyes reflected a great sense of humor. We both broke out in laughter! He insisted that I take his artwork home with me. I still have that picture and poem tucked away in a closet.

I sat with him for a long time and listened to his stories. I didn't have to make conversation . . . he did it all. We became friends that day.

He told me about the days when he hunted deer on his land that bordered the Broad River. He spoke of his home and how he missed it. It was a very small house, but he dreamed of going back home someday. He wanted to return and spend his "last days" there.

The old man had never married. He did have a girlfriend long ago, but it was unclear to me what had happened. As he spoke of the girlfriend, his eyes again reflected his aliveness in the dim light of the convalescent home. He still had a dream that one day she would walk through the doors of the nursing home and together, they would change the course of their lives! They would be married and live out the remainder of their lives in his small home on the Broad River.

I listened for a long time. Eventually, he tired of talking and drifted off to sleep. I left him sitting there asleep in a reclining chair. Loneliness lived in this place, but the old man had a secret . . . he had a dream more powerful than loneliness!

It's been a long time since I have seen Mr. Flemming, but I have thoughts of him often. The mental picture of him is still vivid in my mind.

Dream on, old man . . .

Mr. Jesse

For many years I've thought about the effects of aging. The older I get, the more I believe that it is not the years that make us old. Sure, I can't run as fast as I once did; I can't jump as high as I once did, and I can't play tennis the way I once did—the fact is, I don't want to! With the passing of years, life takes on new meaning and priorities change. Things that were so important in the past now fall by the wayside in a trivial heap. Not long ago this fact was confirmed to me.

We were invited to a family get-together where two birthdays were being celebrated. Both men were grandfathers on each side of the family. With the invitation came a promise of fishing in the farm lake. An hour's drive and we reached our destination and were warmly greeted by family members. Some of the men were already at the lake fishing. My wife and I were taken down to the lake in a pickup truck. I sat on the tailgate holding two rods and reels and a small tackle box. I was a bit anxious since I had not fished for bass in twenty years.

Arriving at the lake, we put our fishing gear into a boat. It was then that I saw Mr. Jesse fishing from another boat, He was sitting tall and proud, casting the line like a pro. Before we left the bank in our boat, I heard laughter and the splash water as the fish jumped several times. Mr. Jesse was ninety-two years old and on the other end of his line was a four-pound bass! He was having the time of his life! I watched in amazement as he reeled in the fish.

And now, we were in the lake—casting, laughing, landing and releasing large mouth bass along with Mr. Jesse. It was a great day of fishing.

On the way home, I thought about the events of the day. I replayed the scenes over and over in my mind. Ninety-two years old and still catching fish? An old man doesn't do that!

But then, who's old?

The Whisper of the Broom-Sage Field

He can't remember when he made the discovery but he knew it was early in life. Behind his home stood towering hills and deep woods. The hills were filled with pine and cedar trees. It was there that he made his annual journey in search of the perfect Christmas tree. Maybe that was the time of discovery. Or, perhaps it was during one of those times when he climbed to the top of the first hill and saw before him a clearing between two hills. There, in the clearing was a large, open field of broom-sage.

In the broom-sage field, there were many rabbit trails. In those days, rabbits were considered to be a luxury food. So, the boy built a rabbit box and baited it with apples. He took the box to the broom-sage field and placed it very near one of the rabbit trails.

The day was cold, and the light jacket he wore did not block the chill of the wind. It was one of those December days when the sun was shining but the temperature had plummeted during the night. He entered the broom-sage field to check the rabbit box. He thought he would sit down and, just maybe, he might spot a rabbit making its way through the field.

As he sat there, a strange and wonderful thing happened. The broom-sage towered above his head and helped to block the cold wind. The sun's rays, filtering through the sage, gave it a glistening appearance as though it had been painted with crystals. The wind pushed the broom-sage this way and that way, and the swaying effect was almost hypnotic.

Then he heard it. It was like a whisper as the wind gently swept through the field of broom-sage. At times, it had a sound like music. And then it would change. It was like the whisper of time itself being caught up and placed in this field for the boy to hear. Imagination ran wild! Questions about life outside the small community in which he was born ran though his mind with the speed of the wind through the broom-sage. *What would he be? What would life hold for him? Where would he end up living?* It was exciting, and yet peaceful, to the young boy.

The rabbit box no longer seemed important. He took the apples he was going to use for bait and scattered them throughout the field. *Who knows? Maybe rabbits really did like apples and would eat their fill without being trapped.*

At the time, the boy did not realize the significance of the broom-sage field. But, as the years passed, he realized it had been a very special place. It was there that his thoughts had been given free rein. It was a place where he heard the whisper of the Creator as He swept through the broom-sage field with the wind.

Tragedy: Loss of the Front Porch

Most homes built these days do not have a large front porch. That's sad. When the front porch disappeared from the architect's plans, something important was also lost to the idea that porches are no longer needed because they do not serve a useful purpose. After all, air-conditioning beckons us indoors in the summer, and central heat invites us inside in the winter.

But there was a time when the front porch served as a gathering place. In the cool of the evening, people would sit in rocking chairs or swings on the front porch. It was a place where enthusiasm was expected and exaggeration was accepted. Ah, yes! And well done they both were! Never shall I forget the tale of the thirty-six-pound catfish caught in the Coosawattee River.

The front porch served as a place for political debate. There were times when it got really "HOT" on the front porch. Elephants and donkeys, Republicans and Democrats and other words that I did not understand were fired with piercing verbal bullets of truth.

Truth? Everyone knew truth, spoke truth, and demanded that their truth be accepted and appreciated. I wondered how they could all totally disagree and yet, all have truth? As a youngster, I enjoyed listening to the verbal bantering!

But for me, the most important thing about the front

porch was the times when the family would gather there. There would be small talk about the day. The weather was always discussed and predictions made for tomorrow. As the sun was setting, conversation would usually end. Each of us would sit in quietness, alone with our thoughts. I remember sitting on the edge of the porch, legs dangling over the side, staring into the deep woods beyond the railroad tracks while listening to the whip-poorwill in the distance, with the reoccurring thought-contemplation—*The future? I wonder what it will bring? maybe.*

Mountains and Their Mystery

Mountains are a part of my life. Their memory always haunts me and will never totally let go. Mountains hold a mystery, They know many secrets. They have witnessed people climbing up their slopes hoping to find something of value, not really knowing what; but still they climb. Mountains observed young boys as they sat on large boulders on sloped ledges thinking about life and what lay ahead. Special places, these mountains are.

My dad and I used to coon hunt in the mountains on cold, wintry nights. You could hear the dogs barking in the distance as they trailed a coon. Crossing frozen streams and climbing higher, there were times when all you could hear was your own heartbeat. Lungs felt like they would explode in the cold winter air. And there were times when I thought my heart would jump out of my body and shout, "What are you doing to me?!"

An axe, a lantern, matches and coffee made up the baggage of such a hunt. At some point we would take a break from the hunt and make coffee using the stream water. We would sit under the canopy of heaven with stars twinkling in some far-off galaxy while we sipped the dark brew. Few, if any words were spoken. Words were not necessary.

The memories of those days warm my spirit even as I write this. My dad was not a verbose man, but the nights spent in the mountains taught me much about a father's love and his desire to share the mystery. Ah, the blessed mystery! Out of the mystery came a depth of understanding and respect for my dad, a man, a remarkable person, whose influence upon my life could not be over-estimated. The mystery of the mountains still calls out to me.

In the New Testament, we find Jesus spending time on mountains. He had great respect for the truth and mystery found there. He would often retreat to the mountain when he had something bothering him, or just to get away, and especially before he had to make decisions and choices. For him, the mountains were special places. He and His Father must have had intimate conversations on the mountains. There is a kind of sacredness, awe, and mystery contained in the mountains that sprang forth from Creation.

There are still some mountains that I long to climb. When I'm in Western North Carolina on the Blue Ridge Parkway and see standing before me "Cold Mountain" in its magnificent splendor, something unexplainable happens. I feel connected to Mother Earth and a part of that which looms toward heaven's gate in all its majesty! But, I know it's not as easy to climb now as it was when I was a young boy. Regardless, there are mysteries still to be learned even if the climb is made within the framework of my own imagination.

Like life itself, mountains stand before us filled with mystery.

The Wilderness

How important is wilderness in our lives? Wilderness does not have to be a negative thing. If we look at the Scriptures, wilderness plays a very important role in the lives of the biblical characters. John the Baptist practically grew up in the wilderness; Jesus often withdrew to the wilderness. After his conversion, the Apostle Paul went into the Arabian Desert for about three years. Places in the wilderness are often identified as "deserted" or "lonely places but they must have served a purpose.

In the movie, "A River Runs Through It," we are told the story about a family who lived in Montana. The two sons, Norman and Paul Maclean, grew up in this area. Their father was a Presbyterian minister. Between the services on Sunday, Norman and his brother Paul would accompany their father on walks along the Big Blackfoot River. It was here that Norman's father felt his soul restored and his imagination stirred. Walking along the river one day, his father stopped and picked up a rock and said to his sons, "Long ago rains fell and mud became a rock. But even before that, beneath the rocks are the words of God. Listen." Norman Maclean was to say later, "If Paul and I listened very carefully all our lives, we might hear those words."

Things happen in the wilderness. Discoveries are made about ourselves and even our relationship with God. Maybe that's why I enjoy fishing in the mountains so much. Some of the wilderness places of my childhood have long since been destroyed by dams and power plants. But I have a new favorite haunt. It is the Big East Fork of the Little Pigeon River in Western North Carolina. In the background stands Cold Mountain. The scenery can only be described as majestic. Even when fishing, I feel that if I listen closely, I might hear the words of God. His creative beauty is everywhere. The wilderness can be a place where the soul is restored and the imagination stirred.

Sacred Places

Are sacred places found only in a church or a church sanctuary? I don't think so. Moses, reared in a palace, eventually finds himself on the backside of the desert tending those stinking sheep. Suddenly, without warning, he runs smack-dab into a bush that is burning but is not consumed by the flames! God speaks to Moses and says, "Come no closer! Remove the sandals from your feet, for the place on which you are standing is holy ground; (Exodus 3:5 NRSV). That is really a sacred place.

A sacred place does not have to be marked by some miraculous event. Every day is miraculous! A sacred place may be where you are at a given point of time in which you have an encounter with God. The very gift of life and breath is a sacred thing. Sacredness may happen in a church service or it could be somewhere else. Unfortunately, in this hurried life, we become numb or insensitive to the Divine Presence. We miss so many sacred events and places. As I think back over my life, I recall some places that I consider to be sacred.

There was Hopewell Baptist Church where my mother was the pianist. At some of the meetings, she would let me (or was it make me?) stand on the piano bench and sing a solo as she played. I was only five or six years old. My memory holds that place to be sacred not because I sang, but because I was allowed to be part of a community of faith at such an early age.

And there was the tabernacle where revivals were

held each year. Henrietta Keel was there, and one night she walked to the platform and sang, "Precious Lord, take my hand, lead me on, let me stand . . ." And the spirit of a young boy was touched by the soulfulness of a dear lady. To me, this was a sacred event.

There was the Louisville and Nashville Railroad depot in Chatsworth, Georgia, where I answered the call to be a minister of the Gospel at the age of thirty-three. The depot no longer exists except in my mind. But even today, it's like the burning bush event, a holy place, a sacred place.

Countless mountain rivers and streams have provided the much-needed quietness where one can get in touch with God and self. Even the water flowing over rocks brings its own message. And the wildlife?, Well, it speaks also. A deer moves across the river in silky silence. You watch but you hear no sound. And the hawk, looming overhead in search of food, provides the backdrop that lets you know that the Creator really got carried away one day as He worked on His Created Order. And yes, every now and then, a trout rises to a dry fly and the events, taken in context with all that is, become sacred.

The organized church and religion have their place in sacredness in their own unique way. At times it may be difficult to identify but it is there if we really look. In this world there are many sacred places if we only have eyes to see them.

The Whittemore Spring

I grew up in a small, rural community. Like most young-sters, I had my favorite places of escape. One such place was a large hill with giant rock formations covering almost all the top of the hill. At the bottom of the hill, there was a big water spring that lay among tall, shady oak trees. It had the coldest, sweetest water I ever drank. A gourd used for a drinking dipper was always placed on the large rock next to the spring. It was not uncommon to find a gallon of milk in the spring, cooling for an evening meal.

The spring provided a place to relax, to cool off from the summer heat. Minnows darted around in the spring as if they were playing games. I spent many great moments at this oasis. It was at the spring that I could give my mind and imagination free rein. I could dream and be anything I wanted to be.

As the years passed, I often thought of the spring. I shared the memory of this place many times with my son, Chris. One day while visiting my parents, I decided to take Chris to this special place. When we arrived at the spring, I hardly recognized the place. How it had changed! Dead trees had fallen. Erosion had taken a toll on the area. Undergrowth had completely taken over. The old trails that I once knew so well were no longer there. We searched the area. "It has to be here, a spring can't simply vanish," I said to Chris. But after searching all the places that I thought it should be, we gave up. It was gone. I had wanted my childhood memory to be a part of my son's life. But it was too late. Disappointed, we left.

Years passed and the spring became a faded memory. One summer day, we were on our way to visit my parents again. It had been several years since Chris and I had searched for the spring. For some reason, I drove by the old spring place again. I couldn't believe what I saw. Someone had done a lot of work around the area. I stopped the car, got out, and looked in the direction of the spring. All the fallen trees had been removed. The undergrowth had been cleared away. Once again, the old place had a familiar look about it. We walked in the direction where I remembered the spring was located. Sure enough, there it was! It had been cleaned out and restored, and it looked as majestic as ever. Memories of long ago flooded my mind. The large rock, now uncovered, looked the same. The only thing missing was the gourd. Even the minnows still darted around the floor of the spring. We lay down on the big rock and tasted the water. It was the same! Cold and sweet as ever.

The Whittemore Spring had been there all along ... waiting to be uncovered and rediscovered. We sat by the spring for a long time in silence. We were fascinated with the discovery of this relic from my past.

As we sat there, a strong impression swept over me. It was as though God were saying to me, "I'm still here and I still love you. But like the spring, your life needs the debris and undergrowth of worldly things cleared away." I determined that my life would thereafter be different.

It was getting late. We had to leave. But before we left, we lay down once more on the large rock and tasted the clear, cold water again, and again ...

A Friend and His Mountains

On vacation, we spent most of our time in the Tennessee and North Carolina mountains. Most of the time was spent in pursuing trout even in the midst of torrential rainfall! But, in spite of the weather, it was a good week. I always enjoy being in mountains that are new to me. Each one has its own characteristics.

It's hard to describe, but there is something about mountains that speak to a person's soul. On one particular day it had been raining most of the time. We were back at the motel after a hard day on the river. I walked out of my room into the parking lot and I saw him. He was my friend and fishing partner. He was standing in the parking lot leaning against the fence looking at the vastness before him. The view of the mountains was breathtaking.

I watched him. He knew the mountains. He grew up in Western North Carolina. Together, he and his dad fished the streams and hunted in the hills countless times. I watched, as he seemed to be caught up in his own thoughts. Ah, the mountains must bring back many memories. Perhaps some hunt that went on all night or some stream where a big brown trout rose to a fly was now making its way through his thoughts. His dad was his hero. He told many stories of his dad's skillful art of fly-fishing. His father, now too old to fish, had been a master fly-fisherman.

In the distance was the imposing Cold Mountain, one of the highest peaks in the area. In WWII, a military plane crashed into this mountain; the plane is still there, it is said. A movie was recently made entitled "Cold Mountain," about people from Cold Mountain who fought in the Civil War.

I did not interrupt my friend, as he stood motionless, caught up in the scene before him. I, too, have felt the power of the mountains. They speak with their own voice. It is a voice of greatness, of strength, of mystery, and at times even loneliness. They stand alone in the midst of a vast wilderness. One wonders what secrets they know. They have seen many people come and go, and they must know many stories of failure and success, sadness and joy, and life and death. To be in the mountains of such magnificence is not a person's right . . . no, sir! It is a privilege.

Tomorrow as we make our way to the streams that are held within the arms of these great mountains, I must remember that privilege. My friend and fishing partner, Gil Massie, knows of this privilege. After all, he was taught by a master fly-fisherman about the Master's Creation.

Old Horizon

A young boy stands on the sandy beach looking out over the ocean. The warm, tropical breeze blows while the waves come crashing in one after the other. He stands with his hands in his pockets, and his eyes are fixed straight ahead. The great expanse of sky and water come together at a point far off in the distance. The horizon is where things come together, but never really come together. With the speed we use to try to capture the horizon, it uses the same speed to move away from us.

"What mysteries do you hold, Old Horizon? What is out there between you and me? Why are you so elusive? If I could make you stand still while I approach the point where things meet, what secrets could you tell me?" The boy has many questions and few answers.

"Ah, lad," says Old Horizon. "Between thee and me there are many mysteries and great truths. But this knowledge comes only as you make your way toward me. For between thee and me there is a lifetime. The great truths and secrets you desire to learn can only be discovered as you live your life one day at a time. Keep your eyes fixed on the horizon, the point where things come together. You are young now and I see the excitement in your eyes as you ponder the things that await you in life. Between thee and me there is much living, learning, and loving to be achieved by you. Keep your eyes fixed on the horizon, the point where things come together."

Old Horizon continues. "And the days will pass

quicker than you think. For between the two of us, tomorrow becomes today, today becomes yesterday, and the cycle continues." The boy asks no more questions of Old Horizon.

Days pass and the young boy becomes a man. His eyes still hold excitement but look tired; the shock of blond hair is now gray; his step is not as quick as it once was. And the day comes when Old Horizon speaks again: "Remember when we spoke long ago on the sandy beach and you had all those questions? I see you have discovered many of the answers. You've had a good life, and you lived each day to the fullest; you learned great truths as you lived each day; and your life has been filled with love. What more could you ask for, my friend? But I see you are tired. The years have taken their toll. So, lie down and sleep, take your rest. You are about to discover the greatest of secrets! When you rise in the morning, you will rise in the horizon, the point where all things come together."

And a young boy stands on a sandy beach looking out over the ocean, eyes fixed straight ahead . . .

The River

It was seven-thirty in the morning. The fog had not completely lifted as I reached the river's edge. It was eerie as I stepped into the cold water. No one was around. The only sound was the flow of the water breaking against the rocks.

Wading into the river to get in a position to make a cast, I could feel my heart beating faster. Overhanging tree limbs and a large rock provided a perfect spot to find a trout. Strange, perhaps, but there are times when you know a trout is present and waiting.

I watched the fly drift downstream under the tree limbs and around the rock. I held my breath. In the quietness of the early morning, I watched and listened and waited as the tiny fly reached its target. *Be ready to set the hook*, I told myself. *Not too quick now, be patient. Wait, wait . . .*

And suddenly the explosion! The early morning came alive with the sound of a rising trout taking a dry fly! Water and spray went everywhere as the trout made his first jump!

Downstream he went, stretching out the line. Given his size and strength, he must have weighed at least five pounds. He had to be taken! No one would believe me if I lost this fish. The drag on the reel screamed as he went downstream, turned left, then right. I tried to work him very carefully because of the lightweight tippet.

At last he was tiring. Reeling the line as fast as possible, the fish was now coming toward me. "Of all the days to leave the net in the car!" I scolded myself. Now the great brown was only about ten feet from me. He lunged again but freedom was not to be found!

"It's almost over!" I shouted as though he could understand me. The great fish, finally exhausted, lay motionless. I reached down to get him but then . . .

The alarm clock went off. It was Monday morning. Soon I would be in a staff meeting at work, but in my mind I would be somewhere else.

Dark Prong

The name is "Dark Prong." It's a small mountain stream that is reported to have brook trout in it. To get to Dark Prong, we had to drive up the Blue Ridge Parkway and park at a place called Graveyard Fields. Dark Prong is nestled deep in the Shining Rock Wilderness area of Western North Carolina. It is a long walk to the stream.

When we arrived at Graveyard Fields, there were a couple of pickups already there. Some hunters had just turned their dogs loose. My partner asked them, "What are you hunting?"

"Bear," they said, "we're after black bear."

High-powered rifles were slung over their shoulders. It didn't take a genius to figure out that we were going to be walking in the direction the dogs had gone. *Um, what if they run a bear in our direction? What good is a fly rod?* I asked myself. So I let my partner go first—just in case. After all, he was much more familiar with the area. After hiking a couple of miles, we reached the stream without a bear incident.

Dark Prong is a beautiful stream. The banks and rocks along the stream's edge were covered in ice. Fishing this stream would be a challenge. Wading less than fifty yards, I found a small pool where the water flowed under a large rock. A perfect place for a trout. I made a cast. Suddenly, a nice brook trout appeared and just as quickly disappeared. I made another cast. The tiny fly floated gently down the current, under the rock—and the brook trout could not resist! He took the fly and no small commotion followed! It was almost a twelve-inch brookie.

We had a great day. We caught and released trout in almost every pool and many riffles. We were so caught up in fishing and in the beauty of the surroundings that we forgot that it was getting late and we needed to start back. In our excitement that morning, we had failed to mark the trail where we had entered the stream. Heading downstream, we knew we had to get to the main river before dark. We didn't realize how far we had fished up the stream. Once we reached the river, we knew there was a hiking trail on the other side that would lead us back to the truck. We had been there before.

Over falls, rocks, rapids, and bluffs, we walked and stumbled, hoping to make the river by sunset. Around each bend, we thought we would reach the main river, but it was just more of Dark Prong that lay before us. The hours were passing quickly! We were bruised and battered from the rugged terrain. I was hurting from the top of my head to the soles of my feet! Our waders were ripped and torn from the sharp rocks and fallen trees we encountered.

It was almost dark when we finally reached the main river. Off in the distance, we heard dogs running and barking as they trailed something. Was it a bear? Crossing the main river, we spotted the "Mountain-to-the-Sea Trail," barely visible in the failing light. My partner was now so sick from dehydration that we had to take a break. We had sipped some water from a small side stream a few miles back, but it was not enough; the dry-heaves were taking a toll on him. He stretched out alongside the trail hoping the nausea would pass. After about thirty minutes, we decided to go on. It was now total darkness as we attempted to find our way along the mountain trail.

Once we made it to the highway, we still had about two more miles to hike before reaching the truck at the Graveyard Fields. When we reached the main road, I heard the words "Thank you, Lord!"

Eight miles we hiked before we reached Graveyard Fields. To make matters worse, a game warden was waiting at our truck. She wanted to check our fishing license.

We were so cold and tired we had a difficult time in just finding our license! Finally, she gave us an O.K. "Have a good evening," she said cheerfully as she was leaving.

"Yeah, same to you, lady!" someone in our party said.

As I reflect on this pilgrimage, I know we were fortunate not to have some serious injuries. In spite of the aches and pains, it had been a great day! Was it worth it? You bet! We had our limit of fish and had kept them cool with ice found alongside the stream.

As I write this now, a year later, we are planning another trip to Dark Prong. However, this time our exit will be by a different route. Not only was there tremendous beauty at Dark Prong, but fish were in good supply—

And God was there, too

Angel in the Whirlwind

It was the Virginia Statesman, John Page, who wrote to Thomas Jefferson after the Declaration of Independence was signed: "We know the race is not to the swift nor the battle to the strong. Do you not think an angel rides in the whirlwind and directs this storm?" President George W. Bush used this powerful quote in his inaugural address.

Whirlwinds and storms go hand-in-hand. A large part of life itself is made up of whirlwinds and storms. The events that are out of our control constitute the storms of life. When bad things happen and we find ourselves helpless to do anything about them, a storm sweeps over us! We pray. The storm passes. Sometimes we survive. Sometimes, people pass into eternity. But through it all, could it be possible that "there is an angel riding in the whirlwind, directing the storm?"

Conflicts arise. People become unreasonable! There is nothing you can do to bring harmony into the situation. Harsh words are spoken! Tempers flare! Worry and sleepless nights abound! Then, in the wee hours of morning while darkness still hovers, the thought comes—"There's an angel in this whirlwind."

Children grow up and graduate high school. Often this event brings with it great uncertainty: turmoil and unrest afflict the family. Decisions have to be made, but no one can agree. There is a storm brewing! But wait—

"There is an angel in the whirlwind . . ."

Retirement. But where did the time go? And so many decisions have to be made! Questions fill the mind—What will my lifestyle be after retirement? Will there be enough money to pay the bills? Can we make it? It's life in the midst of a whirlwind! After much struggle and loss of sleep, the time comes when the turmoil subsides. The decision has been made, almost of its own volition. There is a calm.

Methodist ministers get really nervous at a certain time of the year, especially if they are moving to another appointment. Time comes when one must leave the people he/she loves. Then, there is the other church waiting for the arrival. The minister is emotionally torn apart! Whirlwinds! Storms! Yes! But, "there is an angel in the whirlwind. . . ."

She's weak and barely able to speak. Restlessness lives within her frail body. Death is a short distance away. A lone figure leans over the bed and whispers in her ear, "there is an angel in the whirlwind directing this storm." The storm subsides.

I'm reminded of that old hymn, "Stand By Me." Verse 1 says, "When the storms of life are raging, stand by me . . . when the world is tossing me, like a ship upon the sea, thou who rulest wind and water, stand by me."

There is an angel in the whirlwind. . . .

True Grit

One of Webster's definitions of "grit" is "firmness of mind or spirit; unyielding courage in the face of hardship or danger." Yes, sir; I know about grit! I've seen grit in action. I've read grit. I've carried grit. I've made money from grit!

Actually, what I'm referring to is the first job that I ever had. There was once a newspaper called *The Grit*. I think it was a monthly or a bi-monthly paper. I had a paper route in Oakman, Georgia. It was there that I experienced my first business adventure. *The Grit* provided the community with world news even if it was a month old when they read it. My route consisted of about twenty homes. That was close to being the entire community.

The money was not all that great, but it did provide some spending change. Often, I found it difficult to collect money for the delivery service. There were some interesting people on *The Grit* route.

Mr. Will was a large and robust man, who appeared to be strong as an ox. He usually sported a two or three day growth of beard. It was Mr. Will who often gave me a tip in addition to the cost of the paper. Folks there said Mr. Will was given to gambling and strong drink. I suppose the tip came when he was successful at his pastime. He was always kind to me. In later years, he became a good friend.

Then, there was Miss Edith. She was the "old maid" on the route. Miss Edith was a staunch woman whose disposition was serious, negative, and downright rude most of the time. I always noted that when I arrived at her home, there was a black cloud hovering over her place. I made a mistake one time when I asked her, "How are you, Miss Edith?" Well, she told me. I never posed that question to her again. She always complained about the price of the paper being too high. Most of the time she didn't pay at all because of her latest illness, doctor bills, prescriptions, and other excuses that I've long since forgotten.

There were others that I enjoyed seeing. I looked forward to delivering the paper to Mr. Whittemore. I would stop by his spring and take a long, cold drink of water using the gourd that had been placed there for any weary traveler who had a thirst. He ran a general store and gave me a line of credit for candy, cokes, and other goodies. He was always friendly and on time with his payment.

Miss Hattie was the postmaster and general proprietor of another store. She was a kind lady and would often provide me with a 5-cent cup of ice cream. There were a few perks for delivering *The Grit*.

There were some customers who could not be pleased with anything. Some gave excuses why I should not be paid (one of the most frequent was that the dog ate the paper). Others often said, "Well, I don't have any change at the moment, but I will pay you next week." For some, next week never came!

Down through the years, I have met these folks over and over. Oh, they have different names and faces, but they are still there, very much alive. I guess I am indebted to that first job. *The Grit* gave me some good experience about human nature.

As I reflect on the years that I served as a minister of

the Gospel, delivering a sermon each week plus all the other pastoral duties, I have concluded that anytime you deal with people in any context, a certain amount of true grit is required.

The Request

Standing in the doorway of the office, they introduced themselves. Two sisters from Ohio, who were visiting their brother, greeted me with a tone of uncertainty. They appeared awkward standing there as though they were not sure what to say next.

"Could I help you?" I asked.

"We were just looking for a church in this area. Are you the pastor?" I had come to the office just for a few minutes to bring in an article for the newsletter. I was wearing sneakers, faded jeans, an old fishing cap and a sweatshirt. (The thought came to me—*What do preachers wear in Ohio?*)

"Yes, I'm one of the ministers here. However, this is not my clerical garb. Today is my off-day, and I should be fishing, but I'm not." I don't know why I felt I had to explain to them. Maybe it was because they both looked perplexed and confused.

"We came down from Ohio this week to visit our brother. He's dying. We were looking for a place to have the funeral. We were wondering if it would be possible to have it here?"

"Well, where is his church membership?"

"Oh, he doesn't belong to any church. But, my brother is very religious!" Desperation seemed to be creeping into her voice. "Do you have anyone here who can visit him?"

"Well, sure, we visit. The associate pastor is in a

90

meeting at the present time, and I'm on the way home. Perhaps we could visit . . . "

"Please," she interrupted, "we only live a short distance from the church. Could you stop by for a few minutes?"

"Well, I guess so. What is your address?"

The older sister hurriedly scribbled out the directions to her brother's home. At this point, both sisters had tears in their eyes. We shook hands and they left. Sneakers, faded jeans, sweatshirt and fishing cap went to visit that day. It was a short visit but one that I will not forget. We talked, held hands and prayed. It was an emotional moment.

On the way home, after visiting the brother and family, I thought about the entire incident. Why was this so important to the sisters and the brother? It certainly was not anything I did. As Christians and as members of the Body of Christ, the Church, we are God's representatives. In times of need, it does not matter how we are dressed or how we look, but what really matters is whom we represent.

After all, is not the world our parish?

Memory: A Unique Gift

Most everyone enjoys receiving and giving gifts. There are few occasions for which a gift might not be appropriate. Christmas, Easter, birthdays, marriages, graduations and countless other times are gift-giving events. So many of our gifts have a short life span. Clothes wear out, toys break, and food is eaten quickly! And besides, who can remember what you were given last Christmas?

I was told about a teenager who graduated high school. On the last day of school, the parents had a new BMW delivered to the school with ribbons and all. Well, sure enough, people "oohed' and "aahed" about such a tremendous gift. I suppose most of the students were jealous and wished the car were theirs. But a few years from now that gift will be old, the new car smell will be gone and there will even come the day when the BMW will be in the junkyard—old, worn out, rusty, and probably forgotten.

Special gifts do not have to be expensive. The gifts that I am referring to are "Gifts of Memory." We all have them. Good memories last for years. They do not get old, rusty, or worn out and are not forgotten. Think about some of the good memories you have stored away in your memory bank.

I have some great memories of fifty-five years ago when my dad took me on my first "floating-down-the-river squirrel hunt." It was in an old, homemade, flat-bottom riverboat that we used to float the Coosawattee River.

Then there were the summer days and nights that a group of young boys spent camping out on Talking Rock Creek. We would set out trotlines, limb hooks, and throw lines. Much of the night was spent in "running the hooks" and talking about cars and, of course, girls.

Some material gifts I still remember, like my first Red Ryder B.B. gun. But, most of the finest gifts are not wrapped gifts, but time and presence shared with someone important in my life. How often now do I hear myself beginning a sentence with—"You know, I remember when . . ."

The gift of a memory has no price tag.

The Greatest Gift

Thanksgiving is a season when we evaluate or take inventory of all the things we are thankful for in our lives. We count our blessings; lists are made, and there we have it! All the things we are thankful for are on paper. Too often we put the list away and do not think about it again until next Thanksgiving season. The list does not need to be long. Most of the things we are thankful for are derived from one source. That source is the greatest gift we could ever expect to receive. But so often it's taken for granted.

I'm not sure when or how I discovered it. Actually, we all may have been born with this gift but failed to be aware of it until a later time in life. This greatest gift is inclusive enough to accept many definitions.

The gift manifests itself in various ways. A man is sitting in his recliner and the wife is on the couch. They are watching television. For some reason, the man's attention is distracted from the television set and he looks at his wife, but says nothing. She is beautiful. She sits there so gracefully. He seems to be studying her, seeing her for the first time. His heart is filled with the gift as he remembers and gives thanks for this woman, wife, lover and confidant.

A family sits at table sharing a meal. There is chatter, laughter, and "please pass the bread." The events of the day may be recalled in short story form, and then, more laughter. A child tells his/her favorite thing that happened today. Suddenly, without thinking about it, the room is transformed with the gift. The husband's and wife's eyes meet, and there is a simple nod and a smile. Yes, it is the gift at work.

There's been stress over finances. Concern and worry fill the wife's mind. She can't sleep. *What are we going to do? How will we make ends meet?*

Then, there is a voice . . . or is it a feeling . . . or is it an impression? It's not audible but it seems so real! And the mind is suddenly eased as thoughts of *Don't worry, trust me, I love you. It will work out! I will always be here for you. Go ahead, try to sleep*, replace the burden of worries.

Many other times too numerous to mention, the gift has been at work. This gift is not received through making a deal or purchase. That's why it is a gift, the greatest gift.

It is the gift of love.

There Is a Difference

In today's church, maybe the question should be asked or at least contemplated—"Is the Church converting the world or is the world converting the Church?" There is a purpose for the Church being in the world which God created. God, in Christ, came into the world. Christ ministered in the world. Christ died and was resurrected in the world. It was for a purpose. "For God so loved the world that he gave his only Son, so that everyone who believes in him may not perish but may have eternal life" (John 3:16 NRSV). That, in one short verse, is the crux of the entire matter.

There should be a profound difference between the church and the world. Who is converting whom? My spirit is troubled at times because I ask myself the question— "Am I now irrelevant as a pastor in today's world and church?" Maybe I've grown old and not realized it! Perhaps the times have passed me by and I didn't even see them go!

I've always believed that there is an inherent tension in the Gospel between the call of the sacred and the lure of the secular. Jesus' temptation in the wilderness is one example of this tension. One of the things that greatly concerns me today is the growing attitude that the church should look more like the world in order to attract the world to its doors.

Is our goal simply to make people feel more relaxed and comfortable in our worship services? Is our main goal to entertain people when they come to the worship services?

The church must be relevant in today's world. But in all of our relevancy, there must be a difference. The difference is that Jesus Christ died for us, and through repentance and the forgiveness of sin, we have eternal life. The call to discipleship is a call to serve. It is not a call to success as the world defines success, but to surrender as God defines surrender.

There is a difference.

Losing the Mystery

In a quote from Mark Twain, he has Huckleberry Finn saying: "We had the sky, up there, all speckled with stars, and we used to lie on our backs and look up at them, and discuss about whether they was made, or only just happened." You can hear the rumblings and questions of the mysterious in the soul of young Huck. He did not have a great deal to worry about, but life was always an adventure and a mystery.

We just came back from our vacation to Pennsylvania. We ate at an Amish restaurant. We drove around the Amish farms. The lifestyle was simple. The food was delicious and the people were friendly. Yes indeed, "They had the sky, up there, all speckled with stars . . ."

I have no desire to return to the world of "outhouses," no indoor plumbing, and no electricity. Still, we have lost something along the way while building a thing called progress. Much of the adventure and mystery has been removed from our daily existence. There was a time when things were much simpler and life sped below the speed limit. It was the time before freeways, diesel fumes, Internet, fast foods and shopping malls on every corner. I can remember when we looked up to our leaders rather than being dismayed by their lying, arrogance, and dirty tactics. There was a time when customers were treated with respect. There was a time when companies cared about their employees and a thing called "loyalty" existed. Baseball was still a game. Churches were the central gathering places in the communities. It was the age of innocence rather than the age of information. Everything was not known! Mystery had not been killed. It was there in our minds and spirits, adding zest to life itself.

Like Huck, "We have the sky, up there, all speckled with stars," and there is still time to look up, marvel at the scenery once flung into space, and to stand in awe and ponder the vastness of infinity. And from infinity, there came to be a Garden, and in the Garden was human life that fellowshipped with God in the "cool of the evening." At night I imagine the stars were brighter than we've ever known. God saw all that He had created. "Very good," He said, and the hand of God rested.

In the midst of all the clatter, chatter, and busyness that pervade our lives, there is still time to step back. Sometimes when I look up into the night sky and see the Milky Way, the Big Dipper and the Little Dipper, and I take time to be quiet and think, I find myself in absolute awe at the mystery delivered to us by the hand of God.

In those moments, everything else pales in comparison . . .

Snippets

Snippets? What's a snippet? A snippet is a moment of life observed. Snippets may be burned into our minds as vivid pictures that enrich our lives for years as we recall them. Snippets are stark reminders of the importance of life. One has to look for snippets throughout the day, around every corner. Snippets may be people, places, or things, or the interaction of a combination of these.

I was walking through a Target store the other day looking for something that I needed. I don't recall what it was so it must not have been very important. As I turned the corner of an aisle, there she was. She was beautiful. I watched her reach for a stuffed animal on the shelf. She was about five years old. She hugged that animal as tight as she could and nestled her face against the soft plushy fur. It was a nice snippet.

Once after a wedding rehearsal, I went to the place where some men from the church were cooking their annual B.B.Q. Four or five men were sitting around the cooker. They would work in shifts all night. I stood around for a few minutes and listened. The stories abounded; Stories about hunting in Colorado for elk were plentiful. The fishing had been great also. And just to prove it, pictures were available. There was much hand movement to indicate the size of the fish as the stories were unfolding. Laughter and some unbelief accompanied many of the stories. That was also a nice snippet.

In North Carolina on the Hiwassee River, Gil M. and I were fly-fishing. I watched as he made cast after cast. It was truly a work of art to watch the precision of his casting. Nothing was being said, just poetry in motion. The sound of the river and the long sweep of the fly line going back and forth and then released, served to paint a beautiful, peaceful picture. Ah, it was wonderful snippet.

Our grandson, Colby, was just learning to talk. He ran (it seems he never walked) into the room, took the pacifier out of his mouth and for the first time called out—"Pa, Pa!" My heart melted. So I got out of my chair and together we ran to the kitchen where we shared another chocolate "silver bell." Great snippet.

Checking the email on the computer, there was an email from my dear friend, wife, confidante and love of my life. We were in the process of building a sunroom and doing much yard work. Now I admit, I get a bit hyper and anxious at times. But she reminded me of the things we should be thankful for in the here and now and ended it with "I love you, and I am in love with you." To have someone love you, really love you, and to express it through an unexpected email is a snippet without price.

Snippets can be as close as your very breath and your own heartbeat.

Among Friends

It was a cool night. A group of men had backpacked in to the Chattooga River for a couple of days of fishing. Camped on the bank of the river, the moonlight reflecting off the water provided a mystical setting. As the campfire blazed, the sweet smell of burning wood and the familiar crackling of the fire provided a warm and inviting scene.

Men were seated on rocks and old logs around the campfire. Stories were carefully woven with verbal detail and shared with the group. Often they were prefaced with, "I remember when . . . " There were fish stories, gold panning stories, and other humorous stories that had nothing to do with anything really, but they were told with great enthusiasm and men laughed.

Men from different walks of life sat together staring into the fire and relating memories of the past. The stories were important. Now fishing is just about the most important work a man can do. But, when it's all done and men are relaxing together, campfire stories take center stage.

True to form, embellishing a story was expected and accepted. We heard about the catching of great brown and rainbow trout. There was a story about fishing in weather so cold that the guides of the rod became frozen with ice making the casting of a fly impossible. To thaw out the guides, the rod had to be submerged in the water and then a quick cast made before it froze again.

Near the campfire a clothesline was strung between

two trees. On the line hung wet clothes because several people had slipped and fallen in the river while wading and fishing. Each garment that hung on the line represented a different story. Laughter rang out time and time again, then, settled quietly into the burning embers.

Supper had been consumed with great, gusto! Afterward, compliments were given to the chef; then, "Did you hear the one about . . . " was repeated many times. A fisherman-artist discussed his art; another person was warned about using sharp instruments in camp; and then the question was asked, "Was that you snoring last night? You sounded like a chainsaw!" Laughter again.

And the stories continued late into the night while the campfire burned, and grown men were boys once again. And hearts were warmed. And we all knew we were among friends.

At Day's End

Summer and the first days of hot weather always take me back to a time, a time when all the world seemed innocent. Doors to homes were always unlocked. Only a screen door held shut by a spring attached and secured to the framing on the inside by a small latch held the world at bay while we slept.

Summertime. Hot days. The only breeze produced was by small, hand-held fans with a picture of Jesus on one side and a funeral home advertisement on the other. When the day began to draw to a close, we would find ourselves on the front porch. There were rocking chairs, straight-back chairs, and a swing at one end of the porch. The family gathered here to perform the daily ritual.

As the day was almost gone, with only a hint of daylight left, we sat together, sometimes speaking, sometimes in silence. A question might be asked and answered in a slow, carefree tone. One could call it conversation but it was more like rhythm that had a spoken answer made complete by silence. Words were spoken ... silence ... and then, slowly but surely another word or two and then more silence.

In symphony with this rhythm was the whippoorwill that could be heard from the deep woods across the highway and railroad tracks in front of our home. "*Whip-poor-will, whip-poor-will!*" The strange, sad song of this night bird signaled the ending of another day. Tree frogs, crickets, and locusts often joined in with the song of benediction.

Against nature's musical backdrop was the sound of the rocking chairs that rocked gracefully and readied tired bodies and drowsy eyes for a night's rest. And the "creaking" sound of the swing at the end of the porch that held a brother or a sister or both offered its own form of harmony. And the youngest of the family sits at porch's edge with his feet dangling over the side and waits impatiently for the first lightning bug to appear. "Look!" he says excitedly, "There's one! See? There's another one!" I suspect God smiled. Amen.

And night had come . . .

Once Upon a Time

Once upon a time is a phrase that refers to a time, but no time really. Many of the old stories began with "Once upon a time." When we hear that phrase, we prepare ourselves for a story that may or may not be true. "Once upon a time" there was a little girl named Little Red Riding Hood. Or, "Once upon a time" there was a young boy named Jack, a giant and a beanstalk. These stories carry us back, usually to a time when we were young; a time of innocence, and a time when all was well with the world. We felt safe and secure as the words at bedside began with, "Once upon a time . . ."

Once upon a time there was a watch, a beautiful pocket watch, a Hamilton, 17 jewels. Indeed! It was quite a watch. Once upon a time a man bought the watch and carried it for years. He was smooth as silk in extracting the watch from his pocket. It was second nature to him. He didn't have to think about what he was doing, he just did it. A quick motion of the hand and the watch was before his eyes. At church, he would retrieve the watch with that same quick, fluid motion. It was hardly noticeable to anyone nearby, except to a young boy. Yes sir, the old man knew in a flash if the preacher was on schedule or if he had gone on too long. Most of the time, it was the latter much too long! The young boy worked for the old man in the summer when school was out. It was hard work! He spent many hours in a corn mill with the old man, making meal. The old man had a route that he followed. Together, he and the boy delivered cornmeal once a week to stores from Dalton, Georgia to Cartersville, Georgia. The boy disliked the work. At times he became greatly aggravated with the old man because he was such a hard worker, and he expected the same from anyone who worked for him.

In spite of the hard work, though, the boy had great respect for the old man. He knew there was not a dishonest bone in him. He also knew that he was a man of faith, and he practiced his faith not only in church, but also in his dealing with other people in the community. Many times the boy observed the old man giving an extra measure of cornmeal to those in need.

When the old man died, the watch was passed down to the boy. He never carried the watch but left it in a safe place at home. It was merely a keepsake. He often thought of the old man.

As the boy grew older, the memories of the hard work faded. There came a day when the young adult was cleaning out a cabinet, and found the watch. As he held it in his hands, his thoughts traveled back in time to the old man. It's strange how things change with time. It was not the hard work that he remembered, but rather a work ethic that came to his mind. He recalled the compassion the old man had for others.

His thoughts went back to the "once upon a time" life when he had been in church with the old man. For some reason, music always touched the soul of the old man. The boy remembered watching as tears welled up in the old man's eyes when the congregation sang "Amazing Grace." Often, after the song was over, the old man would rise from his seat and request that the last verse be sung one more time.

For the young man, now twenty-five years old, life

had not been easy. He still had many questions about destiny, purpose of life, and faith. There was a void in his life, but he didn't know how to fill it. Something was missing! Surely there was more to life than what he was experiencing?

Standing in the middle of the room with the watch in his hand, he prayed for the first time in a long time: "God of the old man," he heard himself saying. "If you are real, reveal yourself to me. Forgive me and help me to be more like the old man. Amen."

There were no fireworks or flaming chariots, or a burning bush, no—not even a Damascus Road experience. He had hoped something dramatic would happen, but nothing did. He put the watch down and went to bed disappointed. As he drifted off to sleep, thoughts of the old man occupied his mind.

When he awoke next morning, he had forgotten about last night. As he sat up, he noticed the watch that he had placed on the dresser next to his bed. Picking up the watch, he wished the old man were still here so they could spend some time together. There were many things he would like to say to him. There were questions he would like to ask him.

As he held the watch, the young man slowly began to realize that something was different. He couldn't quite put his finger on it, but something had changed. There was a calm within him that had not been there before. It was a quiet peace, something that had been foreign to him for many years. He was shocked when he heard himself whisper, "Thank you, Lord." At first he was embarrassed. It seemed so unlike him, so unnatural. It felt both strange and wonderful.

Maybe this was the secret the old man possessed, he thought. *Or was this the secret that possessed the old man?* Even the confusion and chaos seemed to have left him. He now had feelings that he didn't understand completely but accepted with gratefulness. It was some time before he could accept the possibility that God had intervened in his life. Maybe it had happened to the old man in the same way in another time? Was that why he was so different? Inwardly he felt that regardless of circumstances in his life, everything was going to be all right. For the first time in his life, he felt that his life was on track. His life did not have to be void or meaningless! The future was before him and today was the first day of a new beginning! He placed the watch back in the cabinet.

Once upon a time, a life was changed. The young man now? Well, he's a retired United Methodist Minister. He still has the watch. It is dented, scuffed up and does not work. But, it doesn't have to work or keep time, because, "Once upon a time" refers to no time really but includes all time. The watch lies on the dresser's edge by his bed. There is nothing magic about the watch, just a reminder of the old man, and his faith, his Godliness, and an event that happened to him—"Once upon a time."

The Blue Heron's Praise

One of my favorite hymns, written by St. Francis of Assisi, is "All Creatures of Our God and King." The first verse of the hymn says, "All creatures of our God and King, Lift up your voice and with us sing, O praise ye! Alleluia! O brother sun with golden beam, O sister moon with silver gleam! O praise ye! O praise ye! Alleluia! Alleluia! Alleluia!"[1] Legend has it that St. Francis could talk to birds and animals. I think that for him, everything in all of God's Creation had a voice to sing praises to the Creator.

Last year while fishing in the Chattahoochee River, we walked to Bowman's Island below Buford Dam. On the way in, my partner discovered a big Blue Heron that had a broken leg. The great bird had managed to find sanctuary in a hole in the bank under a large tree. It must have been in great pain. We went to the fish hatchery and told an employee about the crippled bird and where it was located. The employee knew of two women who made it their job to nourish injured birds and animals back to health. As far as we know, they collected the great bird and repaired the damage. When its health was restored, they released it back into the wild.

Each time we fish the river, we usually see one or two Blue Herons perched on a fallen tree. You can approach them only so close, and then they take flight. Blue Herons

[1]The United Methodist Hymnal, p. 62. The United Methodist Publishing House, 1989.

are magnificent birds. To watch a Blue Heron fly and glide with a gracefulness that only God could create is a wonderful experience. When in flight they will often cry out in their haunting, shrill voice. This majestic bird adds great beauty to the landscape of Mother Earth.

Now, when I see and hear the great bird, I wonder if it was the one that was injured and nourished back to health. It could be that his grace in motion and the shrill voice is a way of expressing his praise to the Creator.

"All creatures of our God and King, lift up your voice and with us sing . . ."

A Forgotten Man?

Most folks want to be remembered. It feels good when people know your name. We work with people daily; we live with people; we worship with people. We share stories of faith and humor, but also stories of troubled times. When things are not going well in our life, we need friends, people to listen to us and share in our journey. We do not want to be forgotten!

When I broke my ankle on a fishing trip, it was a friend who came to my rescue. It was friends in the church who sent cards, made phone calls, and visited in our home. It was friends who kidded me unmercifully! And I loved every minute of it because I knew people cared, and they expressed their concerns in many ways.

There are people who have very little support. Recently I visited a friend of many years standing, who was almost ninety-five years old, and resides in a nursing home in Atlanta. He has outlived his family and most of his friends. He had been a faithful member of his church since he was a young man. For many years he had lived alone. But failing health had made it impossible for him to make it on his own. He may have been physically sick, but his mind was still clear and sharp.

Arriving at his room, I found the door partially opened. Pushing the door completely open, I walked into the room. It had been a long time since I had seen him. I started to speak, but I was so shocked by his condition that I stood there in silence for a moment. Tears were streaming down his face. He was trembling as if he were freezing. He didn't recognize me at first because of his failing eyesight. But as soon as I spoke, he remembered me.

"Mr. C., can I do anything to help you?" I asked.

"No! Nothing! Nothing!" There was anger in his voice. "I called the nurse thirty minutes ago. She said she would be here as soon as she could, but everyone was very busy. It's dehumanizing! That's what it is!"

Holding on to the edge of his bed he spoke in a softer voice, "I tell you, Bob, this may not be a bad place, but it's a sad place."

It was then that I realized his bed needed changing. He was embarrassed and angry. He must have felt as though he was a forgotten person. Regardless of what reality was, he felt helpless, alone, and uncared for by anyone.

I left his room to get a nurse. I stayed outside while the nurse changed his bed and gave him a bath. Afterwards, I visited with him for a short time, but his mood soon told me that he didn't feel like talking. I left but promised him that I would be back soon.

As I waited for the elevator, I remembered how he was once upon a time. He had been a great outdoorsman. He had many stories filed away about hunting and fishing. He loved life and demonstrated it by the way he lived. I wondered, *How does this happen to a person? Does his church know where he is living? He had many friends in the church when he was a vibrant man and full of* life! *Were they doing anything to help him or was he just another inactive member on the roll of the church who could no longer contribute in a meaningful way?*

As I drove home, I was afraid but I had to ask myself, *How many people have I left behind and forgotten about?*

"May God forgive and have mercy upon us all . . ."

The Endangered Species

Concrete and asphalt are the enemy. They don't grow anything but more highways and buildings. With each passing day, the enemy creeps closer, disguising itself in the latest fashion of "progress." Like an erupting volcano that spews forth lava, the enemy consumes everything in its path. Buildings go up, malls are expanded, and what was once peaceful and serene is now rezoned and branded "commercial."

Woods, rivers, and wetlands are all endangered species. We are rapidly losing a part of nature that cannot be moved to another location, or rebuilt at a later date. Woods are a wonderful part of the natural order of things. When was the last time you walked in the woods, slowly and intentionally and listened as the leaves crunched beneath your feet? To be in the woods and to smell the aroma of the rich, moist soil beneath the leaves, the scent of pines, cedars, oaks, and if we are lucky, sassafras, is an experience that is foreign to many people. There are some things that cannot be duplicated with concrete, asphalt, strip malls, and countless buildings.

A friend of mine was out in the woods on a dreary, rainy day. When he came in, I asked him, "Why were you in the woods on a day like this?"

"Oh," he said, "I was just being quiet and listening to it rain."

Ah! Did you hear that. O my soul? Hopefully, we have favorite places where we can go to "get away." A favorite place for me is a hillside that leads down into a valley. The entire area is covered in thick rows of pine trees. I relish the thought of being there on a cold, wintry day in the midst of this sea of pines and to simply be quiet and listen as the wind sweeps through the trees. The cold winds pushing the pine needles this way and that way produce a soft harmonic sound.

Only on a few occasions have I been fortunate enough to be in the woods and watch the drabness of winter turn into magical white as the woods fill up with snow. For a while at least, it is pure white. Not a track of any kind can be seen—just a layer of soft whiteness. It's a miracle! That's what it is! Suddenly, the world is transformed before the eyes. Falling snow is almost an eerie silence, but if you listen closely, you can hear the sound as it gently touches the trees and ground. I expect Robert Frost must have experienced that miracle when he wrote the poem, "Stopping By Woods On A Snowy Evening." He talked about stopping by some woods owned by a fellow who would not mind if he stopped and stayed a while. It was snowing hard, and all he wanted to do was "To watch his woods fill up with snow." So simple, but what a beautiful image!

Woods hold a special place for me. They make me feel connected to God's Creation. They give assurance of belonging to an order that only God could have provided in the beginning. "And God saw that they were good. And there was evening and there was morning, the third day" (Genesis 1:13 NRSV). What a day that was!

The woods and nature are like God talking to Himself, and my how He does go on!

The Power of Imagination

Tiger was my friend. Tiger was a dog, a small dog highly trained in the art of survival. He was a mixed breed with white and brown spots. My sister claimed Tiger as her dog, so I let her think that because I didn't want her to feel bad. But Tiger and I, well, we went through so much together! We traveled extensively in the spring, summer, winter, and fall.

We had a nice backyard at home in Oakman, Georgia. A giant oak tree stood in the middle of the yard. From one of the limbs high above the ground, a long grass rope was attached, and on the other end an old car tire was tied to the rope. It was a wonderful homemade swing where I could swing so high that my toes would touch the clouds! Beyond the yard was the garden, and beyond the garden were woods, hills, and more woods. This was home. This was the place where Tiger and I planned and went through so many hair-raising adventures together—the more dangerous, the better the adventure! Tiger often said, "Let's do something dangerous!"

"Okay," I said. And so dangerous and exciting excursions abounded!

I recall a time when the backyard was suddenly transformed into a prairie where we hunted buffalo. Tiger could track buffalo with great expertise. When he confronted one of these animals, his snarl and growl would make them freeze in their tracks. He always gave me a clean shot! The woods beyond the garden became high country where mountain men roamed and many bad men lived. We fought many a battle there and never lost one! On those winter trips after the battles, Tiger would always snuggle up to me. I knew he didn't like the cold weather of the high country. We lay close together so that we could survive those cold, freezing nights.

We trapped beaver, shot cougar, and once went to Alaska for a polar bear hunt. It was during this hunt that a large polar bear got so close to me that he knocked the rifle from my grasp and was about to do me in when Tiger joined the fight. He fought that bear for hours, and when the victory was his, he dug a large hole and together, we buried that beast!

There was a day in Africa when Tiger cornered a king cobra in the grape vines along the garden's edge. What reflexes! I watched in amazement as Tiger grabbed that snake by the neck and shook it until it was dead! I remember Dad commenting at the supper table that night about a dead green snake he found at the garden's edge. Green snake indeed! My dad knew very little about snakes. Once again the great warrior had saved my life!

And then came a cold day in midwinter when Tiger snuggled up to me as we sat beside the giant oak tree and recounted our adventures. He was very old now. He said to me, "I'm so tired. I just want to curl up and lie here for a while."

"Go ahead, old warrior...take your rest," I said. "You've earned it."

It was getting dark as I went into the house. I looked back once more at my best friend. He was resting well.

When I awoke the next morning, Tiger was not waiting at the back door as usual. He was still asleep! I went out to feed him but he didn't move. Tiger was dead . . . my heart sank, and I could not hold back the tears. Suddenly my adventuresome world came to a crashing end! What would I do without my warrior at my side? I finally came to the realization that nothing would ever be the same again.

We buried Tiger in an old abandoned sawdust pile because sawdust piles generate heat from within. Now, when the cold wind blows and the chill of winter is great, the old warrior can take his rest and will never be cold again.

The Trail

The day was sunny and warm. We were at Gooch Gap. Our intended hike was from Gooch Gap to Neels Gap, some fifteen miles. The Appalachian Trail was before us. Filled with anticipation and a backpack that I wasn't sure I could carry, the hike began.

It was something I always wanted to do, but just never got around to doing. I am convinced that no matter where one starts on the trail, it is always straight up! There is some level ground in the Georgia section but only after you ascend for what seems like an eternity. It wasn't long until everything hurt—legs, shoulders, feet, and lungs. But the body slowly and painfully adjusts. At a certain point, you feel you can hike forever. This feeling soon passes. The trail says, "Easy, huh? I'll show you!"

The trail has magic. It also has a long, historic tradition. No one beats the trail, but it's there so that you can test yourself by taking one step at a time. A blind man and his dog are known to have hiked the entire trail from Georgia to Maine! It seems impossible, but a man named Bill Irwin and his Seeing Eye dog, "Orient," hiked 2,168.9 miles through fourteen states.

The first man to hike the trail was Benton MacKaye. He described the threefold purpose of the trail: "1) to walk, 2) to see, and 3) to see what you see."

The trail allows one to shed the normal hustle and bustle of life. No car horns, rude drivers, or traffic lights are found on the trail. What one encounters are the sounds of your own steps, labored breathing, your heartbeat, and the tension of muscles as you push for the next step. The trail is accompanied by beautiful surroundings, the songs of birds, and occasionally small streams that whisper words of encouragement as you cross over them.

On the trail, we met people from everywhere (hyperbole here). We met people from New York, Illinois, Maine, Virginia, Indiana, Florida, Louisiana, California, Tennessee, and of course Georgia.

I felt I was just beginning to get in touch with Creation and myself when the hike ended. Since then, we have planned other two- and three-day hikes. While the trail is a place of testing, it is also a place of solitude where a person can draw aside "to see what you see."

The book of Genesis has taken on new meaning for me. When God created, He always followed the act with the words, "It is good." One only has to sit at the top of "Blood Mountain" and look out over the valleys and mountains to get a feeling for what God meant. He was right—"It is good!"

First Day

The summer had been long and hot. A hint of fall was now in the air. Plenty of time had been spent in play in the past. But now? It was time for a new beginning. The shopping had been completed. The smell of new shoes and denim jeans filtered through the air as the child dressed for this special day. It was a solemn moment.

You could feel the nervousness, the unknown. A tinge of excitement mixed with fear could be detected. There was very little talk as preparation continued. The brave young soul must have been thinking, "What's going to happen today? What am I supposed to do?"

Finally the time came to leave. "D" Day had arrived as the car backed out of the driveway. Arriving at the destination, it was difficult to find a parking place. Walking through the parking lot, nervous anticipation began to build.

Hand in hand, you enter the building and walk down the hall. You read the names on the doors as you pass by. Finally you reach the assigned room. Together, you walk inside. The little hand you are holding is sweaty. Your heart goes out to the child. You know how the youngster feels because you have been there yourself, years ago, and you remember.

And then the voice, a reassuring voice: "Good morning class. I am Miss Jenny, and I will be your teacher this year. We will be spending a lot of time together, learning and having fun."

You wait until the new student finds a desk and sits down before you leave. As you walk down the hallway alone, you can still feel the pressure of the child's hand in yours. What is that in your eye? It must be a speck or something. As you slowly leave, you realize that the baby you love and left behind is no more. He/she is in a classroom that leads to a new journey in life. There's nothing you can do about it except pray and do your best as a parent. Nothing will ever be quite the same again. Sometimes new beginnings are really difficult!

It had been a hard ordeal for you. Driving home you are aware of the mixed emotions you are feeling. You are both proud and sad. But in your heart, you know there will be many more events such as this because that's the way life is.

The Last Time I Saw Him

Sometimes I think God puts human need in front of us in order to teach us how to be disciples of Christ. "See," He said, "it could have just as easily been you." No single person is immune to human suffering. Regardless of how good our life is at the moment, we could be only one step away from poverty or some other great need through circumstances beyond our control. All homeless people are not bums; all people who ask for help are not trying to con us.

The last time I saw him was on Main Street. He was standing on the sidewalk in front of the post office. It was cold. He had on a church rummage sale coat that was much too large, but he clutched the coat as though it were his only chance for survival. He had been around for many years and the wrinkled face was a witness to his longevity. I knew he needed money, but he dared not ask anyone for help. He was a proud man despite his hard life. I walked over to him shook his hand and placed a few dollars in his palm. He looked at the money, and without speaking, nodded his head as a way of saying thanks.

That was the last time I saw him. He has been gone a long time now, but in a way, he is still standing there. Oh, I've seen him many times since then, but he was in a different place and had on different clothes. I saw him not long ago. He was sitting on the sidewalk beside a busy street. One of his legs had been amputated. He was holding a sign that read, "Vietnam Vet." Another time I saw him at a busy intersection. This time his sign read, "I will work for food."

Now, most of the time when I see him, I drive by without stopping or even giving it much thought. I know all the reasons and excuses for not stopping and many of them are valid.

But still, there are times when I can't help but wonder . . .

Positive Thinkers

Is it difficult to be positive in today's world? Looking at the broad picture, we are acutely aware of terrorists' attacks and ruthless dictators in action. Even in our country, we see greed doing its dirty work in all facets of government, corporations, and even charitable institutions. Words like loyalty, integrity, honesty, and trust have diminished in meaning and importance. For many people the outlook on life leans heavily on the negative side.

Last week my wife and I went to the garden section at Home Depot. We spotted an elderly couple walking slowly down one of the aisles. The man was pulling one of those small handcarts. He walked with the aid of a cane. It seemed to take them both forever to take one step. He must have been close to ninety years old and his wife was not much younger. We finished our shopping, checked out, and got into our car.

It was then that we saw the old man and woman coming out of the garden department. They were still moving with those short, little steps as they came toward us pulling the cart. We watched. We thought about asking them if they needed some help, but decided against it. Something about them told us that they took great pride in doing what they were doing. It took some time for them to reach their car. Loaded on the cart was a small cherry tree. It was about two and half feet tall. Finally, they made it around to the trunk of their car which was parked next to ours. With great effort the old man placed the tree in the trunk. After securing the trunk, he got in the car and prepared to leave. Eventually they drove away with a little faster pace than which he and his wife had walked. As we watched them leave, you could see them chatting and laughing. What could they be laughing about?

Could it be possible that they were laughing about planting this small tree and then watching it grow into a large tree? Whatever their conversation was about, it had to be knee-deep in a positive attitude!

Remember this couple, O my soul . . .

Maybe Tomorrow

Procrastination is a terrible disease. I often put off doing today what I can do (hopefully) tomorrow. Phone calls that should be made today are delayed until another day. Cards and letters that need to be written, or visits that need to be made to let people know we care and are thinking about them, are postponed or never acted upon. Then, we find it's too late! Procrastination produces guilt and guilt produces anxiety and anxiety can destroy many of life's great moments.

A friend related the following experiences:

A member of his church was in the hospital. For several days the minister had thought about him. He knew he should go see him, but he was faced with so much busywork. Sermons, bulletins, phone calls, and other work awaited him. The weekend passed. Now it was Monday morning, and the minister had survived the weekend with the necessary work accomplished. So, in all his piety, he went to the hospital to see the person who had been on his mind so much lately. Approaching the room, he knocked on the door. No response. Opening the door, he saw that the room was empty. He went to the nurse's station and inquired about the patient. "Oh, I'm sorry, he expired at four-thirty this morning," the nurse replied.

Guilt overwhelmed him. What was more important—preaching a sermon in the hope of impressing a few folks, or ministering to a brother who was in great need? The answer was clear. For years he was haunted by this experience. Perhaps acknowledgment of failure was the first step to forgiveness.

He related another story to me. It was late at night when the phone rang. The caller asked him to come over. "The end is near," the voice said at the other end. The end was drawing near for a terminally ill patient who was now under hospice care at home. He quickly dressed and went to her home. He still remembered the time he didn't go when he was needed. As he entered the house her husband led him to her bedside. She was very weak and could barely whisper. "Please pray that I will go home to be with Jesus. I'm so tired," she whispered in a raspy voice.

With faltering words, he prayed, "Lord, may your will be done in this woman's life. She's sick and tired, and she wants to go home." Amen. Within an hour she breathed her last breath. She was gone.

Ah, if we only followed our deep impressions more, or maybe it's learning to listen to the voice of the Spirit, we would know that some things cannot be put off until tomorrow. To do the work of God and be in the Will of God requires us to be willing to respond when the Spirit impresses us to do so. It is so easy to put things off until it is convenient for us.

Maybe tomorrow . . .

The Measure of a Person

It was dark when we arrived. Getting out of the pickup, we felt the cold mountain wind cutting through our clothing. There was silence all around. The light of the full moon filtering through the deep woods was a beautiful sight. We were at Hawk Mountain above Hightower Gap, north of Dahlonega, Georgia. From the bed of the pickup, he retrieved his backpack. Together, we hiked about one-eighth of a mile to the shelter just off the Appalachian Trail. He was going to spend the weekend hiking the trail. His plans were to hike the entire trail from Georgia to Maine at a later time. This was the beginning of his training.

After securing his gear in the rustic shelter, he hiked back down the trail with me to the pickup. I was to drive his truck back to Lilbum, Georgia. As I prepared to leave, I watched him make his way back up the trail until he was out of sight.

As I left the mountain, there was sadness in me. I don't know why. Maybe it was because I had left a friend alone in the North Georgia Mountains, or it's possible I wanted to be on the trail myself. I suspect the trail can be a lonely but revealing place. I know that alone in the woods, a person can hear silence, and silence can be awesome. There are times when a person needs to be alone in the stillness, where time really doesn't matter.

Hiking the trail must be similar to fishing a trout stream in the mountains. Mountain streams provide a place where one can "get away" and take in the magnificent surroundings. Places are rare where one can find a quiet peacefulness or at times wrestle with self and ponder things like destiny, Will of God, and other issues. But they are very much needed in order to deal with issues that go beyond the trivial and mundane.

After my friend arrived home, he gave me a quote by Harold Allen concerning the trail: "Remote for detachment; narrow for chosen company; winding for leisure; and lonely for contemplation. It beckons not merely north and south, but upward to the body, mind and soul."

It is often in these settings where those precious moments are experienced that take the measure of a person.

Life's Sometimes and Other Times

Sometimes I feel like I am on track.
Other times I feel like I am derailed.
Sometimes I feel that I know which direction to go.
Other times I'm not sure if I should even move
    at all.

Sometimes I place my worries and cares in God's
    hand.
Other times I take them back into my own heart
    and mind.
Sometimes I worry over minor issues that are
    unimportant.
Other times major issues are ignored and no
    action taken.

Sometimes I am so happy that I could shout!
Other times I am so sad that I could weep.
Sometimes I can't wait for the time to speak.
Other times I wonder if I have anything to
    say at all.

Sometimes my enthusiasm and emotions get
    the best of me.
Other times I'm calculating and rational to the
    point of coldness.
Sometimes my heart is strangely warmed.

Other times my heart is strangely confused.

Sometimes I know that the world is my parish.
Other times I erect "No Trespassing" signs in
   my life.
Sometimes I hear the voice of God so clearly!
Other times I wonder: "Is it God or my own wishful
   thinking?"

Sometimes I feel that I know so much about life.
Other times I feel that I know so very little.
But, this one thing I do know—
That in the sometimes, and in the other times, and
   at all times, I need Thee, O God.

The Three Mouseketeers

Three men I have known for sixteen years are still my friends, I think. At least, the last time I saw them they were friendly. I don't know if they would admit it or not, but these three still maintain a childlike enthusiasm for life. There is nothing they enjoy more than a good laugh at other people's expense. I do not mean to imply that they are cruel to everyone, because their cruel pranks are reserved for "ministers only." But they have zest for living and because of that zestiness, I have the greatest respect for them. They all live in the Watkinsville, Georgia area (Athens, Georgia being the suburb).

Roy, who is known as "Rapid Roy" is a fitness nut. He is addicted to bicycles—expensive, cross-country, racing bicycles. He has the ability to make a decision in a moment's notice. One day while mowing his yard, he grew weary of mowing. Instantly, he shut down the mower, went into his house and showered. Apparently while he was mowing, he decided that he needed to visit his mother, who lives in Augusta, Georgia. After showering and leaving a note for his wife to tell her where he was, he was off! By car it's only about a three-hour trip. No car for "Rapid Roy!" No sir! Wearing his helmet, his skintight shirt and little pants, he was gone in a flash on his bicycle. Distance means nothing to a real athlete.

Cooper, better know as "Country Club Cooper," is a teacher, coach, and occasionally plays tennis. I suppose he is the most ruthless. One hot summer day when we were playing tennis at the county park, Country Club Cooper returned my serve into the far corner of the court. Some sand that I had not seen was on the court where the ball landed. As graceful as Andre Agassi, I lunged for the ball; my feet hit the sand and skidded out from under me. I was hurt...bad. I couldn't breathe; the breath was knocked out of me. I lay there in agonizing pain. True to form, Country Club Cooper walked up to the net, looked over at me and his only words were: "I'm glad I came to play today. I've never seen an airplane crash before."

Louie's alias is "Lightning Louie." He loves Christmas! He decorates his house to the max! On the roof, he always has Santa, his sleigh and all the reindeer. It's not a small scene; it covers half of his roof. Lights are everywhere—roofline, chimney, windows, shrubbery, doors, and all the trees in the yard. People come from miles around to view Lightning Louie's place during the Christmas season.

One day we all went to Lake Oconee at Country Club Cooper's summer home. The "Three Mouseketeers" decided to take a ride on Country Club Cooper's boat. (Actually, it wasn't exactly a boat but a large "party" pontoon vessel with twin engines.) The men talked their wives into going with them on this excursion. I sat on the front porch and watched the voyagers with much amusement. Chattering and laughing, they were like children with new toys! I heard one of the wives say, "Maybe we shouldn't go out today. It looks like a storm is coming up!"

"Storm coming up? Who's afraid of a little rough weather?" asked Lightning Louie. He held the vessel steady and helped the wives get on board. The engines revved up, producing a high-pitched sound. Not to be outdone, nature revved up the wind a notch or two. Off they went...whooping, hollering, and laughing! I watched as they rounded the bend in the direction of the clouds. The wind really picked up and clouds rolled in quickly. No sooner had they disappeared around the bend than they reappeared coming back, engines running full throttle. By now lightning was flashing (real lightning, that is) with great frequency! Torrential rain was coming down in great sheets! The wind had kicked up a good-sized storm.

Sitting in my rocking chair on the front porch, I watched the Mouseketeers coming to the dock. Lightning Louie stood bravely on the bow of the pontoon boat like an old salty sea captain. His job was to help land the party pontoon boat at the dock. Country Club Cooper tried his best to get the boat close to the dock. Rapid Roy was shouting, "Closer, closer, get it closer!" But the wind blew them away from the dock. The wives of the Mouseketeers were now producing loud screaming! Second pass at the dock, and Lightning Louie was leaning out as far as he could in order to grab the edge of the dock with his hand.

Just then, a great bolt of lightning hit the water not twenty feet from "Lightning Louie." He let out a bloodcurdling yell, reminding me of the old Tarzan movies. I've never seen a man jump so high and scream so loud, which accounts for the name of Lightning Louie being born that day.

It took them two more passes before they were able to land the pontoon boat. All aboard were totally drenched! "I told you there was a storm coming up!" said Rapid Roy's wife.

"But, honey," Rapid Roy said, "it wasn't my idea; it was Country Club Cooper who suggested we go for a spin around the lake!"

"Well, I don't care whose idea it was!" said Lightning Louie's wife. "You nearly killed my husband!" Lightning Louie's hair reminded me of someone who had just stuck a finger in a light socket with the power still on. Lightning Louie himself was strangely silent.

As they made their way up the path to the porch, Country Club Cooper said, "Well, preacher, what were you doing, just sitting here looking at us? I guess you were praying for us, right?"

"No, I should have, I know. But to tell you the truth I was laughing so hard that I couldn't pray!"

More laughing!

"Humph! Some preacher you are! You sat in your rocking chair laughing while your church members nearly drowned!"

Lightning Louie walked by me without looking or speaking. Actually, he had not spoken a word since his feet touched dry ground. He went inside the house, sat down on the couch and turned on the television. When I went inside, I noted with interest that Lightning Louie was watching the movie *The Perfect Storm*.

I thought about apologizing, but I was laughing so hard that I couldn't say anything! Besides, I thought about all the jokes and pranks they had pulled on me in the past, and I decided that this was God's payback on my behalf!

Rapid Roy, Country Club Cooper, and Lightning Louie, the "Three Mouseketeers"—Please call me when you plan another trip to Lake Oconee. I love you guys!

Playing the Game of Hoops!

Why is it that agencies of the Federal Government are so difficult to deal with? For some reason they place hoop after hoop for us ordinary citizens to jump through. They tend to wear on one's nerves to the point that you email your congressman, who by the way, only produces a "form" email in return that does not address your concern.

For instance, you cannot call your local post office anymore (unless you have connections! No pun intended). In Georgia you first have to call an office located somewhere in Florida. When you tell them you want to talk to the local post office in your area, they ask, "What is the nature of your business?" Another question I have been asked is, "Are you a family member of the person with whom you wish to speak?" I give up! Go figure!

Not long ago, I was in the process of trying to replace my social security card that I managed to throw away in an old billfold. I finally received the form by mail to fill out (SS5). They want documents, original documents to prove that I am who I say I am. Who in their right mind would mail in their driver's license or insurance card, birth certificate, or some other important original document that you don't want lost?

Not wanting to choose this route, I went to the local social security office in Tucker, Georgia. A sign on the wall said, "Take a number." No problem. I did. It was number 87. I waited for thirty minutes before I heard a number called. It was number 12. Discarding the number

87 in a trashcan, I went back to the office. It was Monday and I had to be back for a meeting.

When I arrived at the church office, I called information to get the phone number of the local social security office. I dialed the number (actually the number is 1–800-772-1213 if you would like to try this exercise). I waited with bated breath as the phone rang. On the other end was a recording. I listened to numerous menus and finally dialed "0" to talk to a live human being. The real live people were all busy. Finally, a lady answered the phone after twenty-three minutes of elevator music. She was not in Tucker, Georgia. She was in Albuquerque, New Mexico. No surprise there!

I asked her how I could make an appointment with the local social security office to replace my lost card. "You can't, sir," she said. "They do not make appointments for that particular need."

"Well, what can I do?" I asked!

"Sir, my advice to you is to go to the office around 8:00 A.M. They open at 8:30 A.M. each day. You should be able to get in and out in no time." Now that was a great tidbit of intellectual advice.

I had to replace my card if I was ever going to retire. So my wife and I went to the local office in Tucker, Georgia at 8:00 A.M. where a line had already formed. We stood in line until 10:00 before we were able to speak to a representative. It took no more than ten minutes to wrap up the business. Two weeks later, I received my card via the U.S. Postal Service!

The CARD of all CARDS is now encased in plastic and stored in a safety deposit box in the local bank. And the game has been played; the hoops have been jumped through in order to satisfy a bulging bureaucracy that adds so little richness to our lives.

Can Anyone Out There Fix This Phone?

The day began very well. I had my work schedule planned. It was a day for finalizing Sunday's sermon and to make one call to AT&T to get a phone repaired in the church fellowship hall.

The secretary called the phone company and talked to a man named Roy who could not understand how we were listed in the phone directory. Eventually, I got in on the conversation, and Roy transferred me to his superior whose name was Stella. Stella informed me that to have the phone repaired, she would have to get a specialist to call me. The specialist finally called and learned that I only wanted one phone repaired. He informed me that I did not need a specialist. He said I should call 1-800-222-3000.

Mistake, bad mistake!

I dialed the number and Jean answered. She told me that they only did work on phones with two lines, not a single line like ours, and said I should call 1-800-526-2000. Edith's turn now. She said it would cost me a $25.00 service charge plus a "large" amount for every fifteen minutes the repairman worked. So I asked a dumb question: "How long do you think it would take him?"

"Sir, I have no idea," replied Edith. It was then that I muttered something about sending smoke signals rather than phoning. Well, dear Edith referred me to yet another number to call.

I dialed the number, 1-800-247-7000. Linda came on the line. Why, I do not know! "Thank you for calling AT&T. This call may be monitored."

"I certainly hope so," said I with as much love and patience that I could muster at the moment.

Linda asked, "Is it the phone or the line that's causing the problem?"

Agitated now, I replied, "I don't know! That's why I've been calling AT&T all morning! Look, Linda dear, I am a preacher, not a phone repairman!"

"Well sir, if you don't know what the problem is you should call 1-800-555-8111."

A man named George answered. He promptly informed me that he did not handle "in-house" service. (I wondered, *Does he handle out-house service?*) Anyway, George suggested that I call 1-800-222-3000 which was the first number my secretary had called that morning. At this point I had no desire to talk to Roy! No! Never again!

In desperation I dialed "0" and the operator answered. I told her it was an emergency.

"What kind of emergency?" she calmly asked.

I said, "AT&T is driving me crazy!"

She found no humor in this statement. "Click."

Disconnected. So, I reluctantly dialed the number George had suggested. With trembling fingers, I pushed the numbers 1-800-222-3000. It rang. I waited. Then, "Hello, how are you listed?" It was my worst nightmare!

Three hours were spent on the phone with AT&T! It had been an exhausting day. With this kind of service, how do they expect anyone to "reach out and touch someone today?" The sermon? Well, I did have a text cross my mind that day, and I gave it serious consideration. It was on the theme of Luke 9:54: "When His disciples James and John saw it, they said, 'Lord, do you want us to command fire to come down from heaven and consume them?'" (NRSV Translation)

By the way, the numbers have not been changed but the names have been changed to protect the innocent—myself!

Ma Bell, I sure love the way you operated once upon a time!

Theological Embellishment

In the beginning God created the heavens and the earth...then Adam and Eve, and then, COMMITTEES. Well, He had to! After all, how in the world would anything ever be completed without a committee?

One day God came to the "Garden Fellowship Hall" in the cool of the evening to fellowship with Adam and Eve. However, there was a problem—a committee meeting had been held and a decision made without God's approval. God was in charge of all committee meetings, but He had not called the meeting in the first place! It had been a shade tree meeting (The telephone had not yet been invented). The first committee meeting consisted of Eve, and the Serpent. Adam, like so many men, had other things to do, so he wasn't present.

It seems that Eve was unsure of Adam's love for her because she was always asking him, "Adam, do you love me?" And of course Adam's response was "Who else?" So, while Adam was out by the fire-ant hill watching the "Ant 500," Eve and the Snake showed up for the meeting. In a desperate move to win Adam's favor, the decision was made to have a family luncheon in the Garden Fellowship Hall. Everyone was to bring a covered dish . . . fruit would be provided. Well, you know the rest of the story.

The Tower of Babel story (Genesis 11) is a story about a Building Committee completely out of control. The chairperson said, "Let's build a tower that will reach the heavens and let us storm the gates of heaven. We will make a name for ourselves!" However, there was a problem. The committee did not realize that what goes up, must come down. Again, God was in charge of all committees, and He was not consulted. This was the first Building Committee that had a communications problem. It probably would not be the last. Soon the committee was divided and eventually they gave up the building program. The situation was one of chaos and confusion. They ended up each person going his or her own way, thus they were scattered throughout the world. And the best-laid plans had failed.

The moral of the stories? Consult God first. Then, show up for work as He directs.

Early Advice: Make It Plain

Over the years I have been given much advice. Most of it has been good. When I entered the ministry, a friend offered this advice. "Make it plain. You have to feed the giraffes and the rabbits. If you feed only the giraffes, the rabbits cannot reach up that high and they will be hungry. But, if you feed the rabbits, the giraffes can reach down and feed on the food and both will be nourished."

A common complaint among people who attend church (I have been told, from time to time) is that they are not sure what language the preacher uses. Jesus never attempted to use language to impress people with his theological knowledge, but he spoke in simple truths called parables, that got the attention of the people. They are not complicated by long, theological words or phrases, but they go directly to the point that he wanted to make. Jesus was never accused of being verbose!

Preachers and politicians are frequently prone to use flatulent speech. In his book, *Power In Preaching,* W.E. Sangster tells the story of plumber who won a running battle over the jargon of bureaucracy, but his victory can be a warning to all of us. The plumber had written to a Washington department reporting that he had found hydrochloric acid good for cleaning out clogged drains, and he received this in reply: "The efficacy of hydrochloric acid is indisputable, but the corrosive residue is incompatible with metallic permanence."

The plumber sent a postcard saying: "Glad you agree with me."

Another letter came: "We cannot assume responsibility for the production of toxic and noxious residue with the use of hydrochloric acid." The plumber wrote another card expressing his great delight that he had been of some use with his suggestion.

Then the plumber received this letter from the governmental department: "Don't use hydrochloric acid. It eats hell out of the pipes." (Sangster, *Power In Preaching*, pg. 65.)

The use of too many words on a given subject may serve to confuse the message one is trying to convey. I think Jesus was aware of this. May we employ brevity and plain speaking with the same effectiveness as Jesus did.

"Let the words of my mouth and the meditation of my heart be acceptable to you, 0 Lord, my rock and my redeemer" (Psalm 19:14).

Where Are We Headed?

Where are we headed? What will the end be? Each day a new voice arises in opposition to something that affects each of us. Now, I admit that not all the voices are bad. There are social movements that have positive benefits in a world that seems to be spinning out of control. But then there are the fanatics whose only interest is getting their way regardless of how it affects the lives of others.

Jobs have been lost due to a spotted owl. There are many people who oppose controlled burning or cutting of our national forests. The argument is that we must protect what we have. I agree with that, but protection and proliferation come through controlled usage of our products. So now our forests are thick with undergrowth waiting to be destroyed by wildfire that is extremely expensive and difficult to control. One bolt of lighting and zap! They are gone. No control. However, some of these same protesters would have no problem building houses on a natural stream and polluting the stream with runoff.

The animal rights folk oppose the use of animals for food. I remember seeing a professor from some college in California telling the world on television that everyone should be a vegetarian. He and others like him want to put a stop to hunting or using any animals for food. If they get their way, we will no longer have the right to eat meat of any kind. It's not humane!

We are in deep trouble here! There is now a group who opposes the use of any plants for food. They contend that plants have "feelings" which must not be abused. It's just not humane! Okay. So take away the meat and take away all food plants and what do you have left? Milk, eggs, and water? Well, who asked the cows if they wanted to be milked? They should have a choice. After all, cow's milk should be used for the sole purpose of feeding young calves. Who are we to intervene in the natural order of things? And eggs? Do we really want to put chickens through the painful experience of laying eggs so that we can digest them and increase our cholesterol? What are we, barbarians?

We are now left with water. Good old H_2O. But is water not made up of molecules? I feel sure that molecules must have feelings and emotions. We better lay off of anything that is made up of molecular structure if we are to treat everything humanely.

So, no more animals can be used for food or medical research. Plants cannot be eaten because they, too, have feelings. If someone commits a crime with a handgun, the gun manufacturer should be sued for the action of the criminal. This makes about as much sense as automobile manufacturers being sued and held responsible for someone having a wreck and causing an injury. It's not the driver's fault; it's the fault of the car manufacturer for building the thing in the first place. So on and on it goes, and where it stops nobody knows!

Where are we headed? We are headed down the slippery slope of irrational thinking where freedom is being diminished at every turn. A sorry situation, which seems likely to continue until common sense returns to our lives.

A Parable on Being Established

Years ago in the days of horse and buggy, in a rural church in North Georgia, a young man wanted to sing some new songs in the church. He played the guitar, but the people were not open to "guitar music." When the son complained, his father always responded with, "You see, son, we are an established church, and we don't want that kind of music in our worship services."

On the way home from church one Sunday, the family was quiet as they sat in the horse-drawn buggy. It had rained all night and most of the day on Sunday. As the horse and buggy made a turn in the bend of the road, and came to a large mud hole, in which the buggy sank down to its axle. The ruts were soft and deep, and the horse could not pull the buggy from the mire.

Again and again, the father popped the whip and urged the horse to pull harder but it was no use. The buggy was mired down too deep to be pulled out.

The father complained, "I don't know why our horse can't pull this buggy out of these ruts!"

The son calmly responded to his father, "Oh, don't worry, Dad—we're just established!" Ummmm.

The point is that we should not get mired down in a rut to the point that we fail to see other people's viewpoints. Music moves the soul! Music sets the tone for worship. Music can cause the spirit to soar, the heart to be grateful, and the mind to be inspired. Diversity in music is a must if we are to be inclusive and minister to people whose views are not always the same as ours. Diversity is a strength, not a weakness.

It's great to be established, as long as we are not bogged down in the establishment.

Spam Mignon

Spam—that wonderful, all-purpose savior of the indecisive chef! It was a staple during the war years. And for some people, it still is! The only thing that I can think of that comes close to Spam is bologna. I read an article in a magazine that informed me that in A.D. 2003, Spam turned sixty-five years old. Aha! So we have something in common!

Now I've eaten at fine restaurants and some that were not so fine. I've eaten at Greek, Chinese, Japanese, Italian, French, American steak restaurants, and just about any and all kinds of food. Fast foods, slow foods, hot foods, cold foods—yep, I've had them all. I've been to restaurants where the "Server" (no longer "waiter" or "waitress") comes to your table after you finish your meal and states in a professional manner, "I will now go and organize your bill, sir." Count on it! You are in financial trouble when you hear these words.

I think God must have created Spam right after Adam and Eve and then remarked, "That is very, very, very, very good!" After all, Spam is more than food! Spam represents simplicity of life; it represents the age of innocence; it is trustworthy; it is nurturing; it is caring and compassionate, and it gives one the feeling that all is right with the world. I tell you, it is a sad state of affairs when so many young people today do not even know what Spam is!

Then, there are those who make fun of Spam. In

the church office one day, I was mentioning that I had eaten some Spam sandwiches. A certain lady responded to my statement with: "No! My dog won't even eat Spam!" So? What does a dog know?

After describing a delicious meal that I cooked for my wife, Phoebe, a church member was heard to remark something about "Spam Mignon." I know that was a statement of derision, but you must understand that this person had not eaten my Spam meal! For those of you who are ignorant about the value of Spam, here is my recipe for Spam Mignon.

Spam Mignon

1 can of Armour Spam
Spray pan with Pam where Spam will be cooked
Add a dash of soy sauce
Add a dash of garlic salt
Slice Spam very thin and fry to a golden brown
Add your favorite cheese topping
Place one slice of fresh tomato on top of cheese
Place the contents inside a croissant
Enjoy!

If the world would only rediscover Spam, world peace, love and tranquility would be more than an abstract thought.

Simplify, Simplify, Simplify

To simplify life is easier said than done. Thoreau's adage, "Drive life into a corner and simplify, simplify, simplify" sounds good, but it is a most difficult thing to do. Few people have been able to accomplish this task. We live in the "informational age." Many of us suffer from informational overload. There are too many headlines and sound bites bouncing around in our heads. Internet, television, radio, political pundits, talk show hosts, CDs, DVDs, digital this 'n' that—all add to the informational overload problem.

I actually remember a time when life was simple. The workweek was Monday through Friday during the day. Saturday was the time for leisure. Sunday was the Sabbath, when we went to church. Sunday school was at 10:00 A.M. and the worship service was at 11:00 A.M. In Sunday school, we were taught the Bible. We heard the stories of Jesus and the love that he has for each of us. We learned right from wrong, we knew the difference between good and bad, and we were taught to respect our elders.

In those days, we only had one service on Sunday morning. That was sufficient! We heard the sermons, invitation offered, and finally the benediction given. By then, it was about 1:00 P.M. The rest of the day was spent mostly at home. There was a tremendous amount of "porch talk." The front porch had a swing and several rocking chairs. In our community, people would take walks in the cool of the day. Often they would stop by and join us on the porch and talk. Many stories were heard of how things used to be. They would tell of a simpler time in life.

The women would often talk about the new "feed sacks" (mostly hog feed) that had arrived at the general store. They would "oooh" and "ahhh" about the color and the fine print of the sacks, which would eventually become homemade dresses. Dress patterns were always a high priority on the discussion list. The men would talk of feats of strength, speed of cars, or size of fish they had caught on Saturday. Most all of the stories were embellished several degrees.

That was about it—church, work, Saturday leisure, gatherings and stories. I have decided that I am going to "drive life into a corner and simplify, simplify, simplify!" But first, I have to check my email, fax machine, voice mail, missed calls on our cell phones, our church web page prayer requests, North Georgia Conference web page, inner office memos, and other information.

Maybe tomorrow . . .

Things to Ponder
and/or Wonder

I heard Carl Hurley, a very good humorist, say that his wife has a Ph.D in philosophy, and she spends much time in "pondering" things. He said that he wonders about things from time to time, but he never ponders. He indicated there is a difference between the two. She ponders about the great issues such as life and death, the meaning of life, and all those great themes that have not become concretized by hard, cold facts. He, on the other hand, spends time in wondering about things like—"How did they get the white stuff inside those Twinkies?"

Pondering or wondering, the mind is exercised to some degree. Life presents us with many things to occupy our thoughts in the skilled art of pondering or wondering. Someone said, "We live, work, and play on a world that seems to be flat while spending time on trying to understand its roundness." The following are some issues or subjects to ponder or wonder about:

Why do air-conditioners only break down in hot weather?
Why is it that the person in front of you at the checkout counter in the grocery store always has hundreds of cutout coupons?
On a clear day we look up and see the sky is blue. But is it really sky? Is it really blue? Isn't it just looking out into the universe?

Umm, let's see. How far is infinity? How much is infinity? Does infinity have matter?

How did I get here? (The entire process of birth—bringing new life into the world.)

Why am I me and not somebody else?

What is the purpose of my life?

When I am gone, will I leave any significant tracks in this world?

What will it be like at the very moment of physical death?

How long will the sermon last this Sunday morning?

What will I be when I grow up?

When God created LOVE, exactly what was His formula?

When a child is born, is love standard equipment?

When God created fish did He have the concept of "fisher-man" ("Fisherperson") in mind?

Why do they call some fly-fishing "dry-fly" fishing when the fly is in the water most of the time? Isn't a "dry-fly" now a wet fly?

When God gave us grandchildren was He aware that we would go nuts over them?

Why do doctors call what they do a "practice"?

Why do "Forest Service Personnel" stay in air-conditioned offices rather than in the forest?

Why do we call school teachers "school teachers"? Shouldn't it be "student teachers"?

Why do we call a freeway "free way" when just ahead is a tollbooth?

If the earth is constantly turning, how can we be sure which way is up and which way is down?

How long is eternity?

Does God really love me? How do I know?

It matters not whether you choose to wonder or to ponder, there is much in life in which much thought should be given. The mysteries of life are endless. To wonder or to ponder these issues is to begin a great adventure that never ends.

My Friend Henry

Henry is a very special friend. I see him almost every day. I don't know how long Henry will be around. His days are probably numbered. But for now, he's here. I look for Henry each day as I go to work. Sometimes when I pass by his place, he's not at home. Even Henry has to work now and then. Henry is very guarded about his place. It's his space and he doesn't want anyone trespassing!

Lately, I have felt a bit threatened. The other day when I went by his place, I noticed that he had a friend. Friend nothing! They were sitting very close together. I think his friend's name is Henrietta. The thing that bothers me about the situation is that Henry might fall in love with Henrietta, get married, and move to another part of the country. But who knows? They might get married and decide to stay on in Gwinnett County, Georgia, and before you know it, we could have "little Henrys and little Henriettas."

My friend Henry is a Hawk, a beautiful Red Tail Hawk. He is a macho type hawk. He works out on a regular basis. He sits in the trees in the swampy area off Ronald Reagan Parkway. When I pass by his place and he's home, I blow my car horn, and of course, he tips his wing (the right one I believe). I would say that we have a great relationship.

I can't be sure about it, but I think Henry is a United

Methodist. He sits in the same pew (oops, I mean tree) every day. Occasionally, he flaps his wings. The other day I drove by and it was "sprinkling" rain, and Henry and Henrietta were sitting together in their tree with their heads bowed. So one could say they have been baptized by their Creator.

I don't like to admit it, but at times, Henry is a bit flighty. But on the positive side, I think he would serve well on the evangelism committee or maybe the outreach committee. After all, he has already won Henrietta!

He sits tall and proud, chest out, head up. Henry is a majestic creature. God had to be pleased when he created Henry. I'm considering putting him on the prospective "wing roll." If all goes well, I think I'll stop by and give him a pledge card.

Ummmm . . . I wonder if he will squawk?

A What?

Once upon a time, Sam, my brother-in-law, asked me, "When are you planning on retiring?"

"Don't know," said I. "I'll have to look at the financial side of retirement."

"So, when you retire, what are you going to do?" he asked.

"Fish," said I.

"But you can't fish every day," said he.

"Yes, I can!" said I.

Silence. He retreated into deep thought. I could see the wheels turning. So I sat at the dinner table waiting for words of wisdom that I knew would surely come.

"You know those television evangelists?" he asked.

"Yes I do, and no, thank you, I do not want any part of that, no way!" I responded—gracefully, of course.

"Hold on!" said he. "I'm not suggesting that. But listen to this idea." Words of wisdom were now imminent. "Why don't you become a Stream Evangelist?"

"A what? What are you talking about? What is this stream evangelist thing?" I inquired.

He continued, "A Stream Evangelist would be someone addicted to trout fishing. You would wade all the streams you could find. If you met another fisherman while wading, you could preach to him or her or anyone that's nearby. And if there is no one around, you could preach to the fish!"

Wheels still turning.

Yes sir! Stream Evangelist! I can see the order of worship as I speak! The prelude would be selecting the appropriate fly. The welcome and announcements could be something like, "Hey fish, I've selected the right fly, I've matched the hatch, so get ready; I invite you to receive." The music would be the flowing water; the call to worship would be the sound of the rhythm of the fly-line on your first cast; the offertory would be "The Catch of the Day"; the sermon would be filled with words of praise to the Creator for all the fish created; the invitation could be, "Rise Up, O Fish, and take this fly"; and the benediction would be said after you caught your limit.

"Umm, you know, Sam, my dear brother-in-law, I like the way you think."

"Well, thank you," said he.

"Uh, by the way," said I, "how much do you think this stream evangelist job would pay?"

"Oh, I don't really know," said he. "Maybe a fin or two . . ."

Never Go to a Restaurant on Mother's Day!

There was a time when businesses valued the customer, and he was treated with kindness and respect. Could it be that the customer is now "never right?" And besides, who cares? One could easily get the impression that all business owners care about is the customer's plastic. I think that today's philosophy must be: "There are so many people needing our services the individual should be devalued. Forget the frills, the niceties, and all of that! We do not have time to indulge the customer."

I'm talking about restaurants and terrible service! After church on a particular Mother's Day, we made plans to eat out with family and friends. We called "Outback's Restaurant," only to find out they had a two-hour waiting list. So we opted for another well-known dining place. It seemed like the perfect choice—new restaurant, close to home and plenty of seating.

Surprise, surprise! After a two-hour wait, we were seated. Inside the restaurant, it was noted that one large section was closed off. Now that's good planning on a special day! Finally! The waitress brought our tea, cokes, etc. We had to place an order for straws. We had to ask for clean silverware, as several forks still had food particles attached from a previous customer's discarded meal. Good grief! Patience rapidly diminishing, we re-ordered more forks with the request that they be clean. Some people in our party ordered appetizers that never came.

"Are you ready to order now?" she asked with a smile.

"What's the quickest thing on the menu you can bring out here?" I asked.

"Oh—I really don't know, sir, what that would be."

O.K. so I opted for shrimp and a salad with a double order of ranch dressing. Perhaps this confused the server or the establishment. The entrée finally arrived. My order had eight small shrimp. The salad—Where's the salad? It was nowhere to be found. Too hungry by now to make an issue of such an insignificant deletion of food, I ate the shrimp, downed the tea, had an extra piece of bread, and then waited for the dessert order to be taken. Instead, our server brought the salad. That did it! I tried to figure this out. I was now in deep pondering mode: *Let's see, the entrée was brought in place of the appetizer; the appetizer never arrived, the salad came in place of the dessert; I dare not even mention dessert now!*

My final thought was, *Should I tip now or before I never come back?* We asked for the check, paid the bill and got out of there. So much for restaurants on Mother's Day!

"O restaurant! What hast thou done?"

Some Signs Spell Trouble!

Have you ever felt like you should have stayed in bed after a couple of hours at work? There are times when things don't go as planned. We've all had at least one bad day in a lifetime. There are certain signs we can look for that may warn us of an approaching "not-so-good-of-a-day."

For example, you are standing in line at a fast food restaurant waiting to order ham and a biscuit. Your taste buds are doing flip-flops in anticipation! When it's your turn to order you are told, "Sorry sir, we are no longer taking breakfast orders." Oh-oh . . . beginning of a bad day.

You are a minister and you are making an early morning call on one of your parishioners. You're greeted in the yard and while you are talking with him, his dog approaches and mistakes you for a fireplug. Pants leg wet, shoeshine ruined, you try to be cordial . . . but it's too late! Bad day.

The church secretary comes into the office and informs the minister that his wife has transferred her membership to another church. Sign of a bad day.

The church is about to split, and neither side wants you as their pastor. Yep—bad day.

A loving housewife has cooked a great breakfast. Ole' grouch comes in, sits down at the table, looks at the toast and asks, "What is this? A burnt offering?" Sure sign of a bad day.

You are a loving child. It's Saturday and you have the

entire day to play with other children in the neighbor-hood. When you return home, you find that your parents have moved. Another sign.

You are a wonderful, caring, loving, hard-working husband. You come home tired and hungry, only to hear your wife say, "Sorry honey, but your plate has been bro-ken." Bad day.

It's a beautiful day and you are feeling great! You go to the mailbox and there's a letter from the IRS with bold letters at the top that reads "Audit." Bad, bad, day.

The years have passed, wonderful, happy years. Then a letter of invitation from A.A.R.P, arrives and you can't believe it! Where did the years go?

If you are having a bad day, don't fret! I love the phrase in the Bible that says, "And it came to pass . . ." Life is good. The best is yet to come!

Pressure from a
Church Secretary

Duuuhhhhh, I sit here in front of the computer and the screen is blank. Darla, the church secretary, buzzes my office and wants to know if I have an article for this week's newsletter. There's nothing like pressure from the secretary on Monday! Darla is the same person who said to me once when I was bragging that I had all the patience in the world—"Well, you should have! You've never used any!"

"Now, do you or do you not have an article yet? The deadline was Thursday of last week and today is Monday, you know!"

"My dear Darla, I'm working on it even as we speak."

"Fine," she said. If she only knew the screen on the computer is blank.

O.K. Now, let's see ... umm ... well ... screen still blank. Maybe there is something in the files already printed that I could use? I look feverishly through the files.

"Buzz, buzz."

"Yes?"

"Well, where is the article?"

"It's almost done!" I said with great patience. Screen still blank. Let's face it; Monday is not a great day for being inspired. Besides, we had a district ministers' meeting today and we did not get back to the church until

165

12:30 P.M. Those district meetings! They are a pain in the . . . "Buzz, buzz."

"Yes?"

"When will the article be ready?" Darla again.

"It will be ready soon, very soon," with less patience now. Does she not know that I did not get to fish at all last week? Besides, I have not had lunch today; my left knee hurts when I walk; I forgot my vitamins this morning; I did not sleep well last night—and we are out of real coffee in the office. What does she expect?

"Buzz, buzz."

"Yes?"

"So where's the article?" Darla asked again.

"I promise it will be there in five minutes."

Something like, "Oh, good grief!" was heard as she hung up the phone.

Article? You want an article? I'll give you an article!

Article: *"A distinct, often numbered section of a writing; a separate clause; a stipulation in a document; a nonfictional prose composition usually forming an independent part of a publication; a member of a class of things; an item of goods; a thing of a particular and distinctive kind!" (Webster)*

I buzz Darla.

"Yes?"

"Darla, here comes the article. I'm sending it now."

"Well, it's about time!"

"Yes, I know. You see I had a problem with my computer screen, but it's working now." Darla is happy.

I hit SEND on my computer and then quickly exit the building. No more buzzes today!

I wonder if the fish are biting . . .

The Reverend Robot

I read an article about a robot being designed to test clothing for the army. The robot had forty articulated joints that allowed movement and stress testing of the clothing. The robot could walk, bend over, squat, drop to all fours and crawl. It had an artificial skin that was sensitive to changes in temperature or exposure to chemicals. The robot could even sweat!

"Perfect," I said to myself. "Why not design a 'Ministerial Robot?'" Imagine the Staff-Parish Committee writing the factory (after polling the congregation and determining what exactly is a perfect minister), and then ordering a custom-designed robot to fill the bill! Of course that determination could take years to accomplish because a "study committee" would have to be appointed to investigate the plan and then report back to the Staff-Parish Committee; the Staff-Parish Committee would report to the Council on Ministries, and the Council on Ministries would make a report to the Administrative Board, and the Administrative Board would make a recommendation to the charge conference.

If the Reverend Robot happened to be male, he would probably be about 6'4" tall. He would have black hair (and plenty of it! No more partially bald ministers.) He would always dress in a black suit, white shirt, appropriate tie and shiny black shoes (wingtips, no doubt). He would have a deep resonant voice that pleased everyone.

Reverend Robot would never get tired. He would not

need a vacation, or any days off from work. He would be available twenty-four hours a day, if needed. In any given situation he would always look ministerial. No beard, moustache, or long hair ... just a clean, slick, and polished look that indicated preacher man! In his conversation he would always say the correct thing every time. Nothing but compliments would come from this silver tongue-minister. He would probably drive a plain, four-door sedan with black wall tires, but no air conditioning, radio, or CD player. He would not own any fishing gear or any of that other "time-consuming-stuff."

The Staff-Parish Committee, in conjunction with the District Superintendent, would take charge of programming Reverend Robot. He would always be walking around filled with joy and great wisdom and extremely kind even in the most difficult situations. Ah, and could he preach! Well, he would draw great crowds with his slick, perfectly delivered seven-minute sermons. Of course he would never disagree with anyone about anything.

Think about the job description that could be developed. He could be the preacher, janitor, secretary, groundskeeper, recreation director, youth minister, music director, organist and pianist. He would not need a parsonage or a housing allowance. He could take up residence in the church office. And the best part, he would not need a salary at all? Can you imagine how much controversy this fact alone would eliminate? Reverend Robot could be programmed to take up certain issues of life, none of which would ever be controversial. He would always be in full agreement with the majority on any issues that confronted them. He would never need sick days or perks of any kind. Well and good!

However, there is a small problem. There are some

things that can't be programmed—things like heart, compassion, love, and being human and real.

Oh well—at least he could sweat. And for some people that would be enough.

A Recipe for "Feel Good"

It's simple. The recipe for "feel good" calls for Friends, Food, and Story. Mix these ingredients well, and you have "feel good." A wonderful experience can happen if one pays attention and listens.

Recently we met with some friends for a fish fry and ice cream outing. As we sat around eating, "Story" began to happen. Story is important in any setting. Listening to someone's story gives us a greater sense of appreciation for that person. In this backyard setting, short stories were told with added commentary by those who were listening. Story was often accommodated by loud bursts of laughter!

There was a story of a person who was repairing his waders (clothing used for wading rivers while fishing) with "aqua-seal." This is a quick-drying compound designed to patch seams and holes in waders. After applying the "gook" he hung the waders up to dry. He didn't notice that the feet of the waders were touching in places where the miracle patch had been applied. The next time he and his partner went fishing, he began putting on his waders only to find that the feet were stuck together in a solid fashion. His partner rolling on the ground with laughter mentioned something about "I'll wade while you hop up the river. Good luck!"

A snake story was told about a giant copperhead swimming close by the legs of a fisherman. This was topped by another story of an even larger Copperhead striking the fishing rod of a certain fisherman as he made his way down a rocky bank to the river. Oohs and aahs could be heard from listeners. So much for the snake stories.

The subject of eyeglasses and vision—or more correctly the lack of vision—came up. One person was relating the story of how difficult it was to adjust to his bifocals. The spouse of said storyteller chimed in with a professional opinion suggesting that "telescopic" lens would be the better solution to his vision problem.

The term "hour glass" was spoken and I don't remember in what context, but I do remember the response: "Oh, I know some people in this group who had an hour glass figure at one time, but then all the sand shifted to one end."

And other exaggerated stories were told and laughter rang out and the human spirit was fed. In a world filled with "busy things" it's good to step back from the hustle of daily life and take time for togetherness and listen to what's going on around us. If we are lucky, we will hear something that will bring a smile or laughter to our souls.

It's part and parcel of the recipe for "feel good."

Children: The Things They Say and Do!

Children can do and say strange but wonderful things. The honest words they speak can bring tears or laughter to the heart of adults. I believe that there is something of a child's nature even in mature adults (whatever that is). At least, I hope that's true. Children are spontaneous and often brutally honest!

My son, Chris once asked me, "Dad, where did your hair go?" Well, I had to explain to him in great detail that the bald spot was not bald because of hair fallout, but rather it was pushed out by great intelligence coming to the top.

One Sunday morning at church, a father was in panic mode. His son was missing. A quick search did not turn up the missing boy. Eventually he was found hiding in a closet. Why? It was our annual Sunday school "Promotion Sunday" and he did not want to be promoted!

Young children often mislabel ministers. When I was pastor at Watkinsville First United Methodist Church, a mother related this story to me. I was on vacation, and I had arranged for one of the retired ministers in our congregation to handle the service. The parents and child arrived, took their seats in the sanctuary and the service began. At some point during the service, the child noticed that I was not there. She leaned over to her mother and asked, "Mommy, where is God today?"

"Oh, don't worry honey," the mother replied. "He's on vacation this week." (Now that is high cotton!)

Children often get the word "Preacher" mixed up with other words. I was driving by a neighborhood and saw the mother and the children in the yard. I waved, and the children waved back. The youngest child ran up to the mother and exclaimed—"Mommy, I just saw 'the creature' go by and he waved!" (Umm, low cotton.)

Some other issues—Babies, Baptism, and Burping! Now, I love to baptize babies! But one has to be quick and careful. Once upon a time I was baptizing this fine baby boy. As I reached for the water, he burped, *big time* burp! My black John Wesley robe was covered on one shoulder with a white, milky substance. I used more water than normal with that baptism.

Another time during a baptism, the baby I was holding grabbed my glasses and flung them across the chancel rail. The congregation thought that was funny! Then after the baptism, I found my black John Wesley robe was wet in a spot where it shouldn't have been. And the little tyke had not even burped.

During a service when I had just gotten up to preach, I heard a rumbling-rolling noise. A young boy sitting in the rear of the church had managed to bring some marbles to the service. The floor was not carpeted. The marbles had managed to escape the bag they were in, and they rolled all the way down and smashed into the altar. "We welcome to the service today the holy-rollers!" What else could be said?

The ministry? I love it! You never know what to expect. Children make sure of that!

He Keeps Coming Around

There was a time when it seemed he did not come around so often. I really don't mind his visits. But when he's around, he calls attention to himself. I don't like that! Actually, I would prefer that he simply visit for a while, keep his mouth shut, and then retreat to some distant place where he can't be seen or heard.

I guess you could say he is my friend. If it were not for him, I would not be here. We have seen and experienced many things together. We've had good times and times that were not so good. I realize that I owe him a debt of gratitude. After all, he's never done anything to offend me. Oh, sure, every now and then he embarrasses me, but I suppose I should expect such treatment. It's part of his nature. He likes to celebrate and sing little "ditties," and I must confess this gets on my last nerve!

If I were to be honest about the situation, I would have to admit that I am not in total control. I can't control his visits or his lack of visits if he should choose to stop altogether. I know the mind plays tricks on us though. When I was very young, it seemed he rarely ever came around. As I get older, his visits seem to come more frequently. I wonder if he likes me better now than when I was young?

As I think about this character, I find that I really do like him, and I hope he keeps coming around for a long, long time. We are closely related to each other, and his name is "Birthday." I find that I greet him each year with a new perspective and respect for life.

"Welcome ole' friend. I hope to see you again next year."

Knowing Your Limitations

You would think a person would learn over a period of time that some things are better left alone. I've often heard, "A man has to know his limitations." I believe that, but alas, I often forget this great truth.

Not long ago my wife, Phoebe, announced that the "sprayer" in the kitchen sink was leaking. I looked at it. Sure enough, the sprayer in the kitchen sink was leaking. So it was off to Home Depot for advice about leaky sprayers. They had one that was identical to ours. I found a consultant and told him my problem.

"Oh, no problem," he said. "That is very easy to fix."

"Really?" I asked.

"Yeah, all you need is a little gasket to replace the old one. No problem!" he assured me.

Well, I felt encouraged. "Do you have the gaskets in stock?" I inquired.

"Sure do, right over here," as he led me to the gasket bin. He showed me the size I needed and reassured me once more that it was "No problem." I checked out at the cash register and it only cost me twenty-three cents. "Ha!" I said to myself. "And Phoebe wanted me to call a plumber for this small job!"

Arriving home I immediately set out to remedy the situation. I found my faithful vice-grips and started to work. Unloosening the connector, I noted how soft the metal was. "Oops, better turn off the water first!" I muttered to myself as the water sprayed the kitchen floor!

Replacing the gasket, I tightened the connector really securely. *Don't want any more leaks*, I thought. I turned the water back on. Uh oh! I must have tightened the connector too tight. The leak was now a small shower. And the floor was much wetter than it was a few minutes ago. Looking under the sink to see what was making a dripping noise, I discovered that the flexible hose connecting the water to the sink had a small hole in it. Things grew progressively worse.

Off with the water again. I decided to remove the entire faucet and replace it with another one from Home Depot. After all, these things carry a "lifetime warranty." Unfortunately, they did not have one like the one I removed, so I had to upgrade. The upgrade cost me an additional $76.00. It was a beautiful faucet. Phoebe encouraged me (actually demanded) that I call a plumber to get it installed.

The new kit cost me $61.00 for installation. I had worked for three hours in removing the faucet and the plumber installed it in about thirty minutes. Solving the problem of a small leak in a kitchen sprayer now had cost me a total of $137.00, plus the additional twenty-three cents I had spent for the gasket in the first place.

My ego was bruised...Phoebe was less than extremely happy about the entire ordeal. Hoping to ease the tension that Mr. Fix-it himself had caused, I assured my wife that this new, beautiful faucet truly carries a "lifetime warranty."

A man has to know his limitations.

In Memory of "Papa Joe"

In May of 1999, I said good-bye to a dear friend known to us as "Papa Joe," one of the kindest men that I have known. It was Papa Joe who gave me tremendous support in some of the darkest hours of my life. During this time he would drop by my house, ring the doorbell, and, when I answered the door, his only question was, "Are you O.K.?"

My response was usually, "Yes, Papa Joe, I'm all right. Won't you come in?"

His answer would always be, "No, I just wanted to make sure you were O.K."

Papa Joe was my adopted father. We had some things in common. We could both be cantankerous at times but never with each other. He loved a good joke. He was a teller of stories.

Papa Joe went about doing good. He helped people when he saw a need. He was generous with his time, his money, and his friendship.

I taught a Disciple Bible Study series at the church. Papa Joe was always there. In Disciple I, he had a few problems with the study, especially the Creation and Garden of Eden section. For Papa Joe, the real Bible was the King James Version. He cared not for new or contemporary translations. Often when someone would read a section from the New Revised Standard Version, he would say, "Now let me read for you what the Bible says about that section!" And everyone would laugh, knowing that it did not bother Papa Joe at all.

He and his wife (known as "Mama Jo") were members of the church chancel choir. Singing was second nature to him. He often sang in a barber shop quartet.

I will always be thankful that our paths crossed in this life. Because of him, my life and many other lives have been greatly enriched.

I miss him even now.